Praise for *In Trembling Boldness*

"For those of us deeply shaped by the spirit and stories of Jesus, this lovely book is indispensable! And for those who seek genuine illumination and heartfelt inspiration in our grim and dim times, this powerful text is for you! Don't miss it!"
—Cornel West, Union Theological Seminary, New York City

"This new constellation of early Christian scriptures adds brilliant facets to the diamond of divine revelation, waking up those of us who thought we knew it all. Here is a room full of forgotten stories about what it once meant to follow Jesus. Some are so strange that they tell me what a stranger I have become to my own faith. Others are so compelling that they refresh my sense of what this faith asks of me."
—Barbara Brown Taylor, *New York Times* award-winning author of *Holy Envy*

"Those searching for truth, belonging, healing, justice and divine wisdom must read *In Trembling Boldness*! In this tender, surprising, nuanced, complex, and hopeful book, Natalie Perkins and Hal Taussig 'interpret' powerful and too oft unknown wisdom texts from the Jesus movement and share modern-day parables for contemporary life."
—Rev. Dr. Liz Theoharis, co-chair, Poor People's Campaign; director, Kairos Center; editor, *We Cry Justice: Reading the Bible with the Poor People's Campaign*

"A full and open-hearted life—this is what Natalie and Hal invite us to enjoy. To get back to Jesus, or to sit at his feet for the very first time. It is a rich and evocative sit, deeply meditative, reflecting on texts at once ancient and timeless. Oh, how

I'll be preaching these texts, with an open heart and a curious mind and a soul waiting to be taken up, while sipping on new wine in old wineskins that do not burst."

—Rev. Dr. Jacqui Lewis, senior minister and public theologian, Middle Church, and author of *Fierce Love*

"How shall we pray? If prayer is the communing of the deep desires of our heart with the deep desires of the Divine, *In Trembling Boldness* is an extraordinary companion for our contemporary prayer life. Drawing on sacred texts of the ancient Jesus people, meditations found in this book invite us into that world even as they root us firmly in this world in all its wondrous complexity. Here, the Divine does not look away from our sufferings; rather, we find the Divine in the cracks, in the vicissitudes, in the sufferings and joys of our lives. We see ourselves in these meditations. They remind us of the presence of the Divine accompaniment even in most unlikely places. In these pages, we are led by the Divine, who abides 'in trembling boldness,' witnessing to the sacredness of our lives."

—Su Yon Pak, academic dean, Union Theological Seminary, New York City

"This collection of meditations opens the heart to the joy and pain of living. Each meditation invites reflection on the profound ways that the divine is woven together with the ordinary moments of our lives. I found myself deeply moved by the tender intimacy and gracious wisdom contained within these pages."

—Katie Reimer, executive director, World Day of Prayer

"In a wonderful attempt at quenching the spiritual hunger of our time, *In Trembling Boldness* introduces the contemporary world to ancient wisdom; wisdom that at one time guided countless souls. Sprinkled with moments of biblical and extracanonical teachings, *In Trembling Boldness* gifts the world with new reflections of real time scenarios, while also harnessing the voice and instructions of the ancients. *In Trembling Boldness* is a balm of healing to the aching and searching soul."

—Chebon Kernell, executive director of the United Methodist Native American Comprehensive Plan and cultural practitioner and member of the Helvpe Ceremonial Grounds

"There is a joy that exudes from Natalie Perkins's spirit whether she is on or off stage . . . whether she is serving or being served . . . whether she's praying or playing . . . Her heart, her insights, her words, are some of the most well thought out and articulated that I've come across. I do believe you will find great encouragement and inspiration as you now read her words."

—Sandi Patty Peslis, Grammy award-winning singer

IN TREMBLING
BOLDNESS

Books by Hal Taussig

After Jesus Before Christianity: A Historical Exploration of the First Two Centuries of Jesus Movements (co-author)

Meals in Early Judaism: Social Formation at the Table (co-editor)

A New New Testament: A Bible for the Twenty-first Century Combining Traditional and Newly Discovered Texts (editor and commentator)

Marking Loss: Rereading the Gospel of Mark Amidst Loss and Trauma (co-author)

Meals and Religious Identity in Early Christianity/Mahl und religioes Identitaet im fruehen Christentum (co-editor)

Meals in the Early Christian World: Social Formation, Experimentation, and Conflict at the Table (co-editor)

The Thunder: Perfect Mind: A New Translation and Introduction (co-author)

In the Beginning Was the Meal: Social Experimentation and Early Christian Identity

A New Spiritual Home: Progressive Christianity at the Grass Roots

Re-Imagining Life Together in America: A New Gospel of Community (co-author)

Reimagining Christian Origins (co-editor)

Many Tables: The Eucharist in the New Testament and Liturgy Today (co-author)

Jesus Before God: The Prayer Life of the Historical Jesus

Wisdom's Feast: Sophia in Study and Celebration (co-author)

Sophia: The Future of Spirituality (co-author)

IN TREMBLING BOLDNESS

Wisdom for Today from Ancient Jesus People

NATALIE R. PERKINS
AND HAL TAUSSIG

Broadleaf Books
Minneapolis

IN TREMBLING BOLDNESS
Wisdom for Today from Ancient Jesus People

Cover Design by Jay Smith–Juicebox Designs

Print ISBN: 978-1-5064-8574-4
eBook ISBN: 978-1-5064-8575-1

This book draws on surprising, strong, and tender resources from some of the most beautiful recently discovered writings from the first two centuries of writings from Jesus peoples in the near East, North Africa, and Mediterranean. To read more deeply in these ancient texts, most—but not all—of these ancient sources can be found right alongside biblical writings in *A New New Testament: A Bible for the 21st Century Combining Traditional and Newly Discovered Texts* edited with commentary by Hal Taussig published by Mariner Books, New York, NY 2015.

Many of these newly discovered extracanonical materials can be found online. For instance, *The Thought of Norea*, which is not found in *A New New Testament*, can be found by a web search.

MS 1644/2
Bible: Acts. Syria, 9th c.

CONTENTS

CONTENTS

CONTENTS

CONTENTS

Papyrus fragment:
Papyrus Oxyrhynchus 1008

INTRODUCTION

Newly discovered ancient writings of Jesus followers deepen individual spiritual connection and healing today. This book quotes and reflects on a wide range of recently discovered ancient Jesus peoples' writings. Quite spectacular finds of these "new" ancient texts have occurred in the last 170 years, and the twenty-first century has already become one of the most adventuresome and active times for those interested in biblical writings. Newly discovered ancient Jesus peoples' literature has been uncovered and published, and is available online. New historical discoveries about "the Bible" are described in Bibles themselves. For instance, the 2022 New Revised Standard Version of the Bible has more than 20,000 changes in the scriptural texts based on new findings.

Early Jesus group writings invite us into a broad family of Jesus peoples. Whether you have an abiding love of the Bible or have been alienated from traditional Christianity, this greater family of writings unlocks spiritual expansiveness. As these newly discovered writings from earliest Jesus peoples leap from hidden crevices of the ancient world to our twenty-first-century lives, fresh perspectives unfold. This gamut of material introduces supportive and inspiring ancient words from followers of Jesus that sound vigorously wise when applied to life today.

We find biblical phrases right alongside newly discovered ancient Jesus teachings. We see, in surprising ways, how material in and outside the Bible sound and feel quite similar. Ancient writings from Jesus-related groups are like cousins to the Bible. Many were written around the same time as writings included in the Bible. For many centuries these biblical relatives have spoken alongside each other. More parts of people's lives today are touched when the Bible can claim its many cousins.

In the last twenty-five years these writings, relatives of the Bible, have been given the name "extracanonical." Striking and very meaningful extracanonical writings are the focus of this book, and millions of people in the last 170 years have come to love them.

It is up to you how much you want to open your heart to writings by very early Jesus peoples. Each of us (Natalie and Hal) has opened ours. We have made performances, songs, musicals, dramas, liturgies, poems, improvisations, and sermons using hundreds of these writings from the first two centuries of the Common Era. It is up to you whether they belong in your heart, in the beating heart of spiritual communities, or in part of a divine heart linking human beings together.

Each of the nine writings by early Jesus people that we include in this book is briefly described in its own section. Following the description are short reflections for life today that quote a portion of that writing. We trust you will return to these reflections again and again to deepen your spiritual connection and growth.

Papyrus fragment:
Papyrus Oxyrhunchus

THE GOSPEL OF
THOMAS

Where discovered: One of fifty-one found in a rural area near the ancient city of Nag Hammadi, Egypt

When discovered: 1945

Length: 114 mini-chapters over nine pages of modern English with clear introduction and strange tacked-on ending

Interesting fact: *The Gospel of Thomas* was found in 1945 in a jar by farmers near Nag Hammadi, Egypt. Scholars are divided on when it was written, with some pointing to the first century while others push for the second century, and some even the third. Written in Coptic, there's only one full copy. Pieces of this text written in Syriac and in Greek have been found as well. Most of the texts in the jar are copies of earlier compositions.

ABOUT *THE GOSPEL OF THOMAS*

The most dramatic story of discovery of writings from various Jesus movements of the first two centuries was of fifty-one documents. The most famous so far is *The Gospel of Thomas*. Found in the middle of the Egyptian desert in the mid-twentieth century, it took almost 2,000 years to discover this gospel and about forty years to translate it into English and other languages; it now has been read by millions of people around the world. *The Gospel of Thomas* is one of the most popular newer gospels, and many other texts have been found since 1850, mostly in north Africa.

The Gospel of Thomas is given over completely to the teachings of Jesus, containing 114 of his teachings. With no miracles, no story of the crucifixion or resurrection, it lets Jesus do the talking, which is both pithy and deep. It makes a strong case that all one needs to be close to God and to have a full and open-hearted life is Jesus's teaching.

Half of these sayings from Jesus are also in the Bible, whereas the other half are brand new with little connection to the Bible. This gospel is as old as the gospels that found their way into the Bible. What a great way to understand these newly discovered documents as close relatives of the Bible, but also popping with fresh ideas for our world!

What continues to draw people to *The Gospel of Thomas* in our day is the ways that Jesus keeps encouraging people to open their minds and hearts to each other, to nature, and to a divine pulse full of wisdom. It does not teach dogma, nor does it push people to follow commandments. Rather the lively words of Jesus keep inviting everyone toward a realm of God stretched out over the whole world.

Jesus said: "Lift a stone, you will find me there. Split a piece of wood, I am there." (30:2)

Jesus said: Those who seek should not stop seeking until they find. When they find, they will be disturbed. When they are disturbed, they will be amazed, and will reign over all things. (2:1–2)

Jesus said: "God's empire is spread out upon the earth, and people don't see it." (113:3)

The Jesus people of the first two centuries came together at joyful meals. Mostly once a week but occasionally more. Women and men, from many different backgrounds, enslaved and free. At these meals, the mix of people was greater than that at an average meal and they thought of each other as a new kind of family. There really was lots of joy, the conversation was lively, and the wine flowed easily.

And there was one other wild, nearly ecstatic, and often sensuous part of all Mediterranean meals of those centuries that also was a part of these Jesus meals. All meals happened with all participants reclining. Really, yes, they all were lying down on couches of one kind or another, sometimes each person on a couch, and sometimes two on a couch together. No wonder these Jesus people occasionally called these meals "the body of Christ." Jubilant, refreshing, lots of different people, with good wine at hand, good conversation, and real bodily contact.

The Gospel of Thomas has a gripping and moving picture of such a meal by an early Jesus group in which Jesus has climbed up on the couch of Salome, one of his women colleagues.

Salome quickly responds to Jesus as he is climbing up on Salome's couch. "Who are you mister? You are on my couch and are eating from my table." Jesus says to her: I come from the One who is connected to all. I was given some of the things of my Father." Salome comes back: "I am your follower." Jesus says: Because of this, I say: When one becomes equal, one will be full of light. When one is in parts, one will be full of darkness. (61:2–3)

This conversation shows real give-and-take between these two colleagues. They are man and woman, but not in an explicitly sexual relationship. The complexity of this exchange hints that they are teachers, working together as colleagues. What a beautiful relationship model for work and community!

In this passage, Jesus notes the ordinary nature of the realm of God and how it is spread out over the earth.

His followers said to Jesus: "When will the realm come?" "It will not come by looking for it. It will not be a matter of saying, 'Here it is' or 'Look! There it is.' Rather, the realm of the Father is spread out upon the earth, but people don't see it." (113:1–3)

Many New Testaments translate the Greek word "*basileia*" as "kingdom" in "kingdom of God." However, in this ancient context, there were no kingdoms in the Mediterranean or New East because they had all been destroyed by Rome. Newer translations of "*basileia*" to "realm" (or even "empire") align closer to power structures these ancient readers and writers experienced. The translation of the "realm" of God helps understand the expansive, commonplace, and ingrained meaning of the ancient Mediterranean world and brings a clearer picture to twenty-first-century people.

REFLECTIONS FOR TODAY
ON *THE GOSPEL OF THOMAS*

THE LIGHT IS OUR HOME

On the first day in her sophomore class in high school, the teacher asked everybody to say where their home was. For Sophie, that was not an easy question.

She really did not know. She was new in town this summer. And for the past seven years she had moved at least every other year, and when she was twelve they moved twice. Her mom was in the Marines, and that meant a lot of moves. The only places that might have felt like home she had lived in so long ago, they didn't really count. Her dad worked in computer software, so he had some flexibility and worked from home, and was there a bit more than her mom.

As she thought about her new teacher's question about where her home was, it was wherever she and her parents lived. She was happy with her parents. But where home was puzzled her. The teacher was still waiting for Sophie's answer to where her home was. Sophie was a bit embarrassed as a sixteen-year-old to say that her parents were her home. She was old enough that she didn't like the idea that her parents were her home.

Here's what Jesus said was home. He said the light was our home:

If they say to you, Where have you come from, say to them. "We come from the light, the place where the light came into being by itself, established itself, and appeared.". . . If they say to you, Are you the light, say, "We are the children of the light." (The Gospel of Thomas 50:1–2a)

BE PASSERBY

The woman was taking the subway home one day and decided not to put in her AirPods. Ah, her precious distractors that took her out of the world of anxious moments surrounded by too many people, that planted her solidly into her curated song list, or an enlightening podcast. But today was a Saturday and she needed to hear if the train was changing its route as often would happen on the weekends. As she entered the subway car, she passed by a fishing pole and its owner.

"Huh!" she thought to herself. "Where does one fish around here?"

She looked for a seat and saw five empty seats toward the rear of the car. As she got closer, she saw why the seats were empty. A man was sleeping on the floor. She found another seat and sat on the edge, trying to touch as little as possible as she rode. A curly blonde-haired tot, who couldn't have been any more than three years old, bounced onto the train followed by a man who looked to be her father. They sat nearby, the little girl's legs swinging far from the floor.

The child said, "Not cool, man. Not cool."

"Alright, relax," said the father.

The exchange made the woman giggle, although she couldn't see what the little girl was referencing.

The train rushed down the tracks, not diverging from its regularly scheduled stops. She breathed a prayer of thanks for this small mercy as she made her way home. Then she noticed a flier stuck in the corner of a subway ad that read

Jesus said: "Be passerby." (The Gospel of Thomas 42:1)

What Jesus meant by those words "be passerby" could be to simply observe and be present to the small details and the lives around us, those we might otherwise miss during our own journey through life.

THE GOSPEL OF THOMAS'S DEBT-MANAGEMENT PLAN

Kevin and Natasha do not have enough money. Natasha has been ill for most of their eight years of marriage and has not been able to work except for about a year right after their wedding and about six months three years ago. Kevin is a painter but has no car, so sometimes he can't get to his workplaces. They rent a small apartment at the edge of the city and are able to pay their rent most months.

The situation of Kevin and Natasha is not uncommon. For many, the ability to work and earn is declining steadily.

Here is what *The Gospel of Thomas* says:

If you have money, do not lend it at interest. Rather lend it to someone who won't pay you back. (*The Gospel of Thomas* 95:1)

What Jesus recommends for those who have enough, or more than enough, money is different from the money advice today, which has widened the gap between the rich and the poor and caused both the young and the old to fall increasingly from middle income into poverty.

As we reflect on the larger situation of who does and does not have money, it is important to know that while the people of Israel forbade all to charge interest on loaned money, Jesus took this teaching even further: we should not expect poor people to pay us back at all.

WHEN THE RICH HOLD ALL THE CARDS

A story from *The Gospel of Thomas* (65) is like stories in the Gospels of Matthew (21:33–46), Mark (12:1–12), and Luke (20:9–19). The story is about a man who was known for loaning people money and then demanding that they pay the money back with interest. In all four gospels that man bought a whole vineyard and made a deal with some workers that they would work at the vineyard from the beginning to the end of the season, when the owner would take all the grapes from the vineyard.

But the end of the story from *The Gospel of Thomas* is quite different:

When the grapes were ripe, the owner sent a slave to collect the fruit of the vineyard. But the workers beat the slave, almost killing him. The slave went back to his owner and told him what happened. The vineyard owner thought perhaps that the workers did not know the first slave, so he sent another slave. But the workers beat him too. Then the owner sent his son to collect the harvest from the workers. The workers then thought about the fact that the owner's son was the future owner of the vineyard. So they seized the son and killed him. There is a lesson to learn here. (The Gospel of Thomas 65:1–2)

The versions of this story in Matthew, Mark, and Luke end with the hearers of the story yelling at Jesus, trying to arrest Jesus, and worrying about the people defending Jesus. But

The Gospel of Thomas story just ends with the workers of the vineyard in control. This gospel assumes most workers in the vineyard are treated poorly and leaves the story in their hands. *The Gospel of Thomas* ends the story with the assertion that it is teaching a lesson.

There are many sayings of Jesus throughout the Bible that stand on the side of poor people, and this version of the story of the workers in the vineyard by *The Gospel of Thomas* stands alongside of Jesus's sayings in Luke 6:20, 24:

Blessed are you who are poor, for yours is the realm of God. . . . But cursed are you who are rich, for you have had your comforts in full.

Reflect on the fact that in more than half of the US states, most of the people who gather the food from the fields for the general population have very low pay, very minimal places to live as they wander from place to place, and very little health care.

YOU WILL FIND ME THERE

Slowly the deep evergreen forest began to fade a bit. A small stream appeared from the depth of the woods, opening space for a small meadow, in which two badgers sunned and a two-year-old buck rubbed up against a stout trunk. The small stream fed into a tangle of willows and then into a larger stream which spread out into many small rocks that sparkled in the sunlight.

Along the upper edge of the stream three different versions of tiny ruby flowers dotted a very narrow ridge. A fish broke the surface of the water and some lazy clouds played against the mountains above. And before long a speckled duck had landed against the lower bank, while a perhaps imaginary hawk landed on the top limb of a broken aspen with its bark hinting some early yellow.

Jesus said: "Lift the stone, you will find me there. Split the piece of wood, I am there." (The Gospel of Thomas 30:2)

And maybe *The Gospel of Thomas* says: "Look closer at the imaginary hawk, you will find me there too."

Surely another fish jumps—perhaps a brook trout—and no one says anything, because it is too beautiful.

CLAIMING A NEW WAY OF BEING SAVED

Emerald had lost her way. Actually, it was worse than that. In these last eighteen months it felt like she had lost her *self.*

How could that be? When she had graduated from college almost three years ago, she was so excited. She felt "grown-up" for the first time in that final year of classes. Then, to get a job that she really liked was a dream come true. She and her girlfriend got an apartment together. Only three blocks from the park.

As she looked back, it was probably when her mother fell that a feeling of danger first snuck into her mind. Her mom was who Emerald depended on, and that fall affected Emerald too in that her mother wasn't available to take walks nearly as often. Then her girlfriend lost her job. Next someone broke into their apartment and stole some money.

And then came the COVID-19 pandemic! Luckily Emerald kept her job, but had to do it from home. That put the two of them on top of each other in ways that did not help. COVID-19 lasted so long. There were lots of moments when it felt like the world was falling apart. Where was her mom when Emerald needed her?

Her work boss was getting mean. Emerald felt like he did not understand what it was like for her as a young Black woman. He had quickly moved toward threats of firing her. And her girlfriend was not supportive either. By that time, she could feel herself slipping further into anxiousness. She had a hard time sleeping and started to worry about money. When her girlfriend suddenly moved out, Emerald was lost.

Out of nowhere, her mom dropped by. She was still walking with a cane. She had found something called *The Gospel of Thomas* at the library and thought Emerald might like a short saying from it. Emerald and her mom read the quote twice out loud. And then together.

Jesus said: "When you give birth to the one within you, that one will save you." (The Gospel of Thomas 70:1)

She reminded her mother how great she had felt less than two years ago, and told her that now she sometimes felt she had lost that real person within her. They took a walk in the park. Slowly. Could she still give birth to the real person inside her?

Emerald listened to Jesus from *The Gospel of Thomas* as she walked in the park with her mom. She was glad that her mother recognized this crazy mix in her life of good and hard. She heard from this remark that there was something within her that could save her in the difficult path of these last two years. She also felt something within her that still knew she was the woman who had learned so much in college and who had kept her job.

THE NAP MINISTRY

It all started because Tricia Hersey was exhausted. This was not how she wanted to live her life. So, she created The Nap Ministry. She says "rest is resistance." Her work can be found on most social media platforms. She invites us to examine our relationship to productivity and worth, our relationship to work and capitalism, and to consider that rest is active resistance and an act of resistance, particularly for Black bodies, against systems of oppression. She calls us to notice that rest is a choice we can make to disengage intentionally from these systems.

> *Jesus said: "If you do not fast from the world you will not find the realm. If you do not make the sabbath a true sabbath, you will not see the Father." (The Gospel of Thomas 27)*

According to Jesus, Tricia is really onto something! The current societal model maintains that there is never enough time to stop and rest. Capitalism fights hard for each individual's attention with devices, apps, alerts, advertisements, and more that continually vie for time. A few years back, one CEO of a very large company literally said, "Our biggest competition is sleep." Restorative rest is antithetical to their goals.

Pulling away from the world allows for discovery. Setting aside real time away to rest allows space to see a little more clearly and to realign from the call of the world back toward the call from God.

TELLING THE TRUTH

An economics podcast did an episode about truth. The host had an interesting way of looking at truth and said: "There are always two truths, the one you say aloud and the real one."

For instance, you are invited to a party. You don't really want to go. You tell your party-throwing pal: "Oh, I can't that night. My daughter has a big recital coming up and I need to be home that evening in case she needs help preparing."

Your daughter does have a big recital coming up, but there's other time to help her prepare. You don't have to help her at that exact time. The truth is you don't want to go.

We tell pseudo-truths all the time. We even do so on a deeper internalized level, in our spiritual lives, shifting our focus from what is real in our hearts. "It's not me; it's them," becomes our viewpoint.

In progressive Christian spaces this pseudo truth-telling sometimes shows up as well-meaning cishet* white folks who are deeply heartbroken about one societal issue or another, yet who have not reconciled their own place in systems of oppression; or those who only want to fight "the powers that be" of the world and are unable to have a conversation about anything else; or those who like the nice, neat package of what church looks like with important causes to fight for in great need of help and support.

Perhaps you've seen this pseudo truth-telling in yourself, and are ready to refocus and admit: "It's not them, it's me."

---

*cisgender and heterosexual

Jesus says: "Those who know all, but are lacking in themselves, are lacking all things." (The Gospel of Thomas 67:1)

Ask yourself: What is it about this particular cause that draws my heart in?

Once you hear your heart's reply, ask yourself: "Why?"

Keep pushing until you get to the root, to where it gets personal. You may or may not like the answer; perhaps you'll find out you do this to avoid pain, guilt or shame, and vulnerability. Or maybe it's to feed your ego, or because you are lonely, or to soothe an old emotional wound that hasn't healed. Whether or not you like what you uncover, whether you like the real truth, finding this answer allows you to not only work on your bigger truth in a fuller way but gives space to work on your real, inner truth as well, gifting your entire work with more authenticity, depth, and meaning. Your work can be more meaningful when you recognize that knowing yourself more deeply connects you to the greater community and work at hand. You need yourself to do this uncomfortable work so that your contributions to the greater good are more purposeful.

RECONNECTING HEAD AND HEART

Zion had been feeling out of sorts for a while now. He hadn't been able to shake it. He was in an "I hate everybody" mood that was completely abnormal for him. Now, granted, it had been one helluva pandemic. Chicago was entering its most beautiful season, showing off all the tremendous colors of autumn; meanwhile everyone around seemed to be at their breaking point. A lot of unresolved trauma from all the death, isolation, sickness, and fear they'd all been surrounded by.

He thought he was doing just fine—talking with his therapist, making sure he was getting all of his creature comforts met. But what he found out was that he wasn't tending to his heart. On a cognitive level, he understood everything, as much as one can, that was happening around him. He was processing new information. But he wasn't tending to the emotional toll this entire thing had taken on him. "When's the last time I cried?" he thought. Sure, he always found pockets of joy, but how much of that was so he could avoid feeling sadness? Apparently, he had reached his breaking point.

Jesus said: "Blessed is the one who has labored and has found life." (The Gospel of Thomas 58)

He took a deep breath as he looked at all the pieces that made up his mental and emotional lived reality. Facing his discovery of a perpetually breaking heart was uncomfortable. While there is no easy fix for this, becoming aware lifts a weight from the shoulders. Knowing our need to reconnect head and heart, he breathed a little deeper, slept a little better. Perhaps this was the first step in finding life again.

JESUS AND FASHION

The dress is lovely and fits great! The skirt is particularly fun in motion.

Although many can argue that these luxury brands are just expensive because of the name they carry, designer brands have a very noticeable quality set apart from those you'll normally see.

Look extra chic for girls' night out. Ruffled long-sleeved jumpsuit! V-neckline and billowing long sleeves with button cuffs.

If you have a luxurious taste, then look into the most expensive clothing brands for men. Over the past decades, designer men's clothing has been getting a lot more popular.

A little romance goes a long way when it comes. Follow one's heart to this ivory lace sleeveless wide-leg jumpsuit! The sleek women's jumpsuit begins with adjustable spaghetti straps and V-neckline. The fitted bodice boasts princess seams and a sultry sheer mesh back with stunning lace-like embroidery.

This fine silk tie stands out with rich hues and a classic grid pattern. 100% silk. Dry clean only. Imported. Tailored fit polo sweater is expertly made from a luxe.

Elegant gold floral printed dress shirts. Crafted from hand-selected material, the long-sleeved shirt has been elaborately tailored.

Timeless silhouettes, warm fabrics, the energy of the city. The winter collection, shot on location in Montreal.

Beyond Paris specializes in athleticwear that empowers you to feel your very best. Using only the finest quality fabrics, the label creates luxe, butter-soft pieces that are made to last.

> *Jesus's disciples said: "When will you appear to us, and when will we see you?*
>
> *Jesus said: When you strip naked without being ashamed, and take up your clothes and put them under your feet like little children and tread on them. Then you will see the Child of the Living One and you will not be afraid." (The Gospel of Thomas 37)*

Many of us in the twenty-first century have a different way of dressing than Jesus and his people did.

MORE THAN TEAMWORK

Those who interacted with small children regularly between 2006 and 2016 probably know all about the animated children's show called *Wonder Pets.* In each episode, a collection of classroom pets—a duck, a turtle, and a guinea pig—went on adventures to save the day by helping animals in need. The majority of the show was sung, like an operetta, complete with a ten-piece orchestra. One of the tunes they sang regularly was when they needed to work together.

"What's gonna work? Teamwork! What's gonna work? Teamwork!"

Parents, teachers, babysitters everywhere could be heard singing this tune with a little one to help them remember to work together.

One of the sayings in *The Gospel of Thomas* is

Jesus said: "When you make the two one, you will become children of humanity. And if you say: 'Mountain, move away!' it will move." (The Gospel of Thomas 106)

Sure, this brings to mind passages in our Bible—in Mark and Matthew about telling a mountain to move with faith the size of a mustard seed. It also sounds a bit like Ecclesiastes 4:9–12 NRSV:

Two are better than one, because they have a good reward for their toil. For if they fall, one will lift up the other; but woe to one who is alone and falls and does not have another to help. Again, if two lie together, they keep warm; but how can one keep warm alone? And though one might prevail against another, two will withstand one. A threefold cord is not quickly broken.

But there is more here in *The Gospel of Thomas* passage. Jesus is talking about becoming one—which is further than the call from Ecclesiastes or even the Wonder Pets. It is further than the side-by-side work of social justice. This can be read as *at-one-ment*, as an amends that must take place. It re-members and reconnects what was once dismembered and broken. When this atonement occurs, a different level of family is achieved. Only then is the impossible suddenly possible.

GOD'S REALM SPREAD OUT ON THE EARTH

Jesus said: "The realm of God is spread out upon the earth, but people don't see it." (The Gospel of Thomas 113:3)

In the trees, birds are singing. A gentle breeze caresses our faces. A four-month-old child coos on the rug. A butterfly balances on the edge of a flower. Crowds pour into the art museum to see a new exhibit.

A young grizzly cub toddles along behind its mother. A couple cuddles in the warm summer evening on the top row of the baseball stadium. Three orchids deepen their hold in the rainforest.

Four twelve-year-olds have fun with their multiplication tables. Stormy waves crash onto a deserted beach. A family pauses on the street corner to talk with a neighbor. Feisty red and blue hummingbirds vie for a place around blossoms.

An eighty-two-year-old widow catches her breath on the bench, contemplating the massive mountain above her. Hundreds of worms produce soil in the meadow. Seventy singers are as loud as they can get.

Papyrus fragment:
Padua Aramaic papyrus 1

THE THUNDER: PERFECT MIND

Where discovered: One of fifty-one found with Nag Hammadi collection in the ancient city of Nag Hammadi, Egypt

When discovered: 1945

Length: Four significant chapters of poetry with one appendix

Interesting fact: The many "I am" statements in *The Thunder: Perfect Mind* are the voice of a divine person. They are very much like the many sayings of "I am" in the Gospel of John. For instance, Thunder says: *"I am the learning from my search . . . I am the one who prepares the bread and my mind within."* (4:10a, 25a). Jesus says in the Gospel of John: *"I am the living bread that has come down from the sky"* (6:51a).

ABOUT *THE THUNDER: PERFECT MIND*

The second most famous of these ancient texts, newly discovered by Egyptian farmers, is *The Thunder: Perfect Mind*. Artistic communities around the world have catapulted *The Thunder* to notoriety. The epigraph of the novel *Jazz* by Nobel Prize–winning author Toni Morrison is taken from *The Thunder*. Umberto Eco discusses *The Thunder* in his novel *Foucault's Pendulum*. Julie Dash's award-winning feature film *Daughters of the Dust* opens with almost five minutes of citation from *The Thunder*. Ridley and Jordan Scott's short film for Prada, "Thunder: Perfect Mind," features this poem for the entire six-minute advertisement. Julia Haines's musical score for the entire text of *The Thunder* has been internationally featured for the last two decades. You'll see some of these featured texts below.

The Thunder features a mostly female divine figure who speaks in the first person. Several sentences show the character of this person both as a divinity and as mostly female. This deity goes back and forth between being revered and humiliated, loved by some and hated by others, or even hated by those who claim love and loved by those who claim hate. The text forces the reader to see complexities next to each other and, in doing so, breaks down the cultural walls society has built about how people are defined. For example, Thunder is described as "he the mother"—showing that Thunder is genderfluid.

> *I am the first and the last*
> *I am she who is honored and she who is mocked*
> *I am the whore and the holy woman*
> *I am the wife and the virgin*
> *I am he the mother and the daughter*
> *I am the limbs of my mother*
> *I am a sterile woman and she has many children*
>
> (1:5–7)

Also of note is the way Thunder calls into conversation with each other the many roles assigned specifically to women—women who are strong and divine but also mocked, the whore and the holy woman, the wife and the virgin, women whose bodies may not match the gender assignment on their birth certificates—inviting readers to examine the stereotypes and ironies of these cultural boxes and opening up room for critique of the limitations and sometimes damage caused by subscribing to these labels. Thunder's work to undo widely accepted views of women and their identity in society allows for reinterpretation of these paradoxes.

Another fascinating dimension of Thunder's divinity is her vulnerability:

> *Do not be arrogant to me when I am thrown to the ground.*
> *. . . Do not stare at me when I am thrown out among the*
> *condemned. Do not laugh at me in the lowest places. Do*

not throw me down among those slaughtered viciously. . . .
I am she who exists in all fears and in trembling boldness.
(2:12–15, 18)

This vulnerability from a divine being is mirrored in the Gospel of John. Both divine figures—Jesus in John and deity in Thunder—present as simultaneously divine and humiliated. However, the self-proclaiming voice in John only deals with glory whereas Thunder's statements mix pain with glory. We can imagine that associating the divine in this way would have provided a closeness to life's real challenges, hopes, and heartbreaks for its ancient audience and provides an entry point for us today.

REFLECTIONS FOR TODAY ON
THE THUNDER: PERFECT MIND

I AM THE MIND AND THE REST

By age sixteen Lillian, a lefty, was riding high. She was completely entranced just to draw, paint, and design imaginary houses, real animals and people, and clothing. Because she had good grades in high school, by the time she was graduating, she had decided to enroll in a college-based fashion design program. By the time she graduated college, she had double-majored in business and fashion design. Her first full-time job came quickly thereafter.

She had a serious car accident her third year in the business and was laid up for four months in rehab and at home. The automobile accident had left her leg permanently lame and her face quite distorted, yet she was able to come back to work part time, although she missed being able to throw herself into the work she prized because her leg remained painful and difficult.

At the same time she returned to work, she fell seriously in love. Her new lover stayed with her and their relationship deepened.

Then her brother, with whom Lillian was close, fell into deep depression. She spent more time with him, although it placed some tension on both her job and her relationship with her lover. She wondered whether she should launch her own design company and work from home.

Before she could decide to launch out on her own, her boss proposed that she become one of the main fashion designers for the business. Lillian was thrilled about this but had to explain to her boss how much her leg was in pain and how the distortion of her face from the accident did not make her feel like a fashion leader. "Just thirty years old," she clarified, "and I already look like a freak show." But it was clear that her boss really wanted her, adding: "Lillian, you can work at home anytime you want" and offering a decent pay raise.

So Lillian managed to be proud of her success, even when many days she did not feel like she could even walk up the stairs to her new office. Freak or not, she loved her work, was happy with her lover, and was glad that her brother now lived in the same apartment house. Although during the next two years she found it increasingly difficult to walk and her leg very painful, her life was extremely rewarding. She experienced increasing renown as a designer and a growing sense of self-worth.

One night coming home from work, her leg gave way under her and she fell down a flight of stairs, damaging her other leg and her right hand. Since her left hand was her drawing and painting hand, her design skills were mostly still there. But after extensive physical therapy she was still unable to walk, and her pain had increased. As she, her lover, and colleagues struggled to think about her future, it became clear to everyone who mattered that Lillian was an extraordinary person and consummate professional. She had not lost her spirit, but she wrung with ache, agony, and throbbing.

"Who am I now? What does my life mean now?" she asked herself.

These eleven sentences from the ancient poem of *The Thunder: Perfect Mind* name Lillian's deep spirit:

> *I am the mind and the rest*
> *I am the learning from my search and the discovery of those*
> *   seeking me. . .*
> *I am . . . the power of powers in my understanding of the*
> *   angels who were sent on my word . . .*
> *I am a foreigner and a citizen of the city*
> *I am being*
> *I am she who is nothing . . .*
> *I am the coming together and the falling apart*
> *I am the enduring and the disintegration*
> *I am down in the dirt and they come up to me . . .*
> *I am she who shouts out and I am thrown down on the ground*
> *I am the one who prepares the bread and my mind.*
> *   (The Thunder: Perfect Mind 4:10–11, 14, 20, 24, 25)*

The powerful, tender, and vulnerable divinity in Thunder can be seen as Christ-like. It is important to note that Thunder's closeness to strength, humility, and tenderness has a bit of Jesus in what is alive in this 4:10–11, 14, 20, 24, 25 section.

PAY ATTENTION TO ME

It was Alberto's normal workday. Get up at five. Throw on some clothes. Grab a couple of leftover tortillas for the road. Up the hill and into town. Cross the main street and walk for seven blocks. Give the usual wave to the older woman opening up the coffee shop, who always waved back. He knew he had to hurry a bit to get to the corner where he and his fellow workers met the truck picking them up to ride to the garden where they all worked.

He made it with a good five minutes to spare this morning.

But none of them were there. There were always some there, but not today.

When the time for the truck came and went without either his colleagues or the truck, his latent anxiousness snapped into real worry. Most of the crew at the garden did not have proper papers, including Alberto. Had they all been picked up by the police?

Should he leave to be sure that he wouldn't be picked up?

Just then he saw a police van turn the corner, driving very slowly. The driver kept cruising, but stared intensely at Alberto. When he rolled down the window Alberto avoided his glance. He felt like running. But where would he run to?

Then he remembered the woman at the coffee shop.

The police van had turned the corner and might be circling around to come back toward Alberto. So with the coffee shop just two-and-a-half blocks away, he made a dash for it. And he got in the coffee shop door without seeing the police van.

Although the shop was not yet open, the older woman who always waved back quickly let him in.

> *Pay attention to me. . . . Pay attention to me, to my impoverishment and to my extravagance. . . . Do not be arrogant to me when I am thrown to the ground. . . . Do not stare at me when I am thrown out among the condemned. Do not laugh at me in the lowest places. Do not throw me down among those slaughtered. . .*
> (*The Thunder: Perfect Mind* 1:3; 2:11, 13–15)

This is a reminder that Jesus people were chased by police for no good reason, as many today are also chased. Jesus, too, was thrown down viciously (Mark 14:65; Matthew 27:26). The Apostle Paul was thrown in jail for no good reason many times (Acts 28:30; I Corinthians 15:32).

Alberto was trying to hide from the police's attention and was able to get away because the coffee shop lady paid attention to him.

Like the character of *Thunder* in *The Thunder: Perfect Mind* and like Jesus, Alberto knows what it is like to be thrown to the ground, to be condemned, and to be in the lowest places. Thunder, Jesus, Alberto, and the Apostle Paul are the people to pay attention to. They point toward a kind of spirit and divinity that also knows what it is like to be thrown to the ground and be in the lowest places.

WHEN THINGS GO WRONG

Frustrated, Daniel put his head in his hands and tried to concentrate on his breathing. He could feel his heart racing and his frustration turning to anger. Why didn't things ever turn out right for him? How come things never seemed to go in his favor? Regardless of all the careful planning he'd done the last year, he was now nearly penniless and alone in a strange city, having left home and moved thousands of miles away for a job that no longer existed. He had been so excited when he booked his first big production contract. His family was so proud. He'd scrimped and scraped to save enough money to make the move, bringing only two suitcases on the long bus trip.

Friends welcomed him to crash on their couch while he searched for an apartment. They told him he could stay as long as he wanted. However, once he arrived, their constant arguing drove him to apartment hunt almost immediately. Daniel was able to find a place pretty quickly with time to move in before rehearsals started. The thousands of dollars security deposit he paid the landlord was more than he expected. He purchased an air mattress online, made a trip to Goodwill for essentials, and figured he'd furnish his place slowly once he was receiving pay from the show.

Rehearsals had been a whirlwind and opening night arrived before he knew it. The show got rave reviews! There was even some Tony nomination buzz. He had managed to purchase a bed and a couch on a payment plan and had been making his payments on time. It all seemed to be coming together, and

Daniel felt proud of how he was figuring everything out on his own.

Then at the top of the new year, the producers called a company meeting. The show would be closing. Though the show sold out every night, the pandemic had so greatly impacted finances, it was impossible to maintain the run. They couldn't afford to keep it open during the slow season before spring break tourism picked up.

That was three months ago. Rumor was that the show might reopen, but nothing was concrete. Auditions for other shows were slow. He'd run through all of his savings. He subbed for dance classes and also worked at a local restaurant. The restaurant kept him fed, but the two jobs combined didn't cover his living expenses.

He sat on the couch with his head in his hands, his stress level high. "What am I going to do?" He felt angry with God for giving him this dream only to have it dissipate almost as quickly as it had materialized. "Hellooooooo, God! Are you even there? I could really use some help here," he prayed.

I am he from who you hid
And you appear to me
Wherever you hide yourselves, I myself will appear . . .
Receive me with understanding and heartache
Take me from the disgraced and crushed places
(The Thunder: Perfect Mind 3:16–18)

The world of an actor can be tough. There are so many uncontrollable variables at play in any given contract. Even when all is going according to plan, situations like this occur all the time. Many Broadway shows did not survive the pandemic, and forty percent of Broadway's talent left New York for good, frustrated with an industry that they'd poured their lives into while feeling little to no return. Perhaps many of them prayed angry prayers, just like Daniel's, to a God who was screaming right alongside them.

A REGULAR DEITY

Jen lives in California with her husband, who drinks too much, and their five-year-old daughter named Wren. She and her husband had just gotten to the point of dealing with his unhealthy relationship with alcohol.

Then Jen's doctor called.

Jen's doctor told her it was colon cancer.

Jen is now the record holder for the most polyps removed from a colon at the center where she was being treated.

Jen was scared.

Jen didn't know what to do.

Jen has a five-year-old daughter whom she wants to watch grow up. She wants to live.

Jen's doctors suggested a total ileostomy. So did the doctors she asked for a second and third opinion.

Jen would have a colostomy bag attached to her for the rest of her life. But she knew she'd do anything to stay on this earth with Wren. Still, she was terrified.

Jen tried to stay levelheaded. She tried to stay rational. She tried to stay positive. She enlisted her friends and family to create a support system. She researched the best doctors. She made her mental health a priority, too. She tried to make peace with losing organs, with losing literal pieces of herself.

Jen's surgeon said she'd rebuild Jen's rectum, giving her the best quality of life going forward.

Jen was relieved. She felt like she could see the path to recovery.

Jen's doctors biopsied her colon and rectum, they studied her chest x-rays and found suspect nodules on her lungs. They diagnosed her at stage three. She would need to start chemo, which meant delaying the second surgery to remove the stoma. She was terrified. Would she be nauseous? Lose her hair? Be so sensitive to cold that it would feel like it burns?

Jen felt guilty. The polyposis syndrome she has may be something she has passed on to her daughter. They'll want to start genetic counseling with her at age eighteen.

Once Jen gets through all of this, she will have an eighty-nine percent chance of living five more cancer-free years. She has no idea how her body will handle all of this, but she is willing to face it with all the courage she can muster. She wants to be here to help Wren grow up. She is scared. She doesn't know what to do. She is face to face with her own mortality, but she keeps fighting for her life. She keeps fighting for each additional day she can get.

Jen is a deity. Not a major deity. Just a regular old deity like everyone else, as Thunder refers to deity and women. The voice of Thunder says:

> *I am she who exists in all fears and in trembling boldness*
> *I am she who is timid*
> *And I am safe in a comfortable place*
> *I am witless, and I am wise*
>   (*The Thunder: Perfect Mind* 2:18b–19)

Maybe Jen is this kind of deity. Maybe we all have been, at one point or another, in our own ways, full of fear as we take the next trembling step. After extensive research, maybe we still feel as if we don't know enough. The God who breathed life into us, who is in us, walks these uncertain steps and takes that next shaky breath too.

SHE LOVES ME

Tears streamed, hot, down Lexi's cheek. There had been some sort of intervention downstairs, all for her, led by her church pastor. But, ultimately, by her father. She had been wrestling with God for such a long time, she'd been studying, she'd been praying, she'd been listening. And when the answer came back as clear as day, she was so excited! During Wednesday's midweek service, when the time came for testimonies, she spoke about the goodness of God and how God has seen her through a particularly difficult time of discernment. But now, on the other side, she could proudly claim that she was gay. The sanctuary fell quiet. Though she didn't remember her church ever talking about sexual identification, this was not the response she was expecting. Usually praise reports were met with jubilance. Lexi sat back down, feeling the heat of embarrassment rise up her neck and burn her ears. On the ride home her parents were quiet.

Later that night she heard her parents whispering in their room. She knew it was about her.

On Friday Family Game Night, the pastor stopped by for a visit. She felt her anxiety mounting all through dinner as she picked at her pizza. She'd lost her appetite. Instead of games, Mom suggested they go to the living room to talk. The pastor started in, saying one thing after another that made her more and more uncomfortable. He told her that at fourteen, she couldn't really know about her sexuality and to give it time. "Sure, I've never even had a first kiss," Lexi said boldly, "but I know what I like." She watched his neck turn red as he told her she was headed for a life of sin. He told her that her sexuality was not from God. Finally she couldn't take it anymore and spouted: "If that's who God is, then I don't believe in God." She felt tears stinging her eyes as she ran from the living room and up the stairs, slamming the door. She heard her father ask the pastor to leave.

Her mother knocked gently. "Can I come in?" After being granted entrance, her mother sat at the foot of her bed. "We just don't want your life to be any harder for you than it has to be," she said.

"Mama, can I show you something?"

"Sure, baby, what is it?"

Lexi pulled up an ancient text she'd been reading online. She'd stumbled across it in a Prada commercial and was intrigued to find more. She pointed to this line:

I, I am without God
And I and she whose God is magnificent.
(*The Thunder: Perfect Mind* 3:13)

"I don't think that God is like what Pastor Steve said downstairs. I don't believe that. I do believe in God, Mama, just not a homophobic one. I think God is bigger than anything we can ever imagine. I think God made me exactly as I am. And She loves me."

BEATEN UP, BEATEN DOWN

It was about ten o'clock at night, and he was on a side street. He heard their feet coming up from behind him. And he started running. But they were closing in. He turned the corner and ran in the street as they closed in. They caught him and threw him to the ground as he yelled for help.

How many times had this happened? He could not remember. But he kept yelling. And they started beating him.

On at least one level he wonders if something Divine is with him at these moments. And he is beginning to realize that the only way something Divine would really be with him is if that Divineness would understand what it's like to be beaten up so regularly.

As they were beating him, he did not hear a whisper of such Divinity. But what did happen was neighbors from a half-dozen houses heard his cries. They came running out onto their porches and scared his attackers away.

That beating did hurt. Some blood on his head. Some bruises. Mostly, an uptick in his fear. At the same time that his neighbors had rescued him, this time hinted at some vague relief alongside the fear.

The next morning as he came down the stairs and flopped on the couch, trying to soften his aches while sipping a hot chocolate; he noticed a pamphlet with a funny title on the table. "Be careful," it read, "don't ignore me. I am the first and the last."

He set his hot chocolate down to read.

I am she who is honored and she who is mocked. . . . I am a sterile woman and she has many children. . . . I am the silence never found. . . . Do not be arrogant to me when I am thrown to the ground. . . . Don't laugh at me in the lowest places. . . . I am she who exists in all fears and in trembling boldness . . . (The Thunder: Perfect Mind 1:5, 7; 2:1, 16)

He picked up his hot chocolate again and thought about this voice he was reading. This was what he had wished for—a divine whisper about fears and trembling boldness. A Divinity that knew who he was "thrown to the ground" and "in the lowest places" (*The Thunder: Perfect Mind* 2:12, 14). This voice was a Divine Lady. But it did remind him of some story of Jesus on the cross yelling like him: "Why have you forsaken me?" A Divine person like him?

A PRAYER FOR BLACK WOMEN

God of our weary years
God of our silent tears
Thou who has brought us thus far on the way
Thou who has by thy might led us into the light
Keep us forever in the path, we pray.

Negro National Anthem

I am she who is revered and adored
And she who is reviled with contempt

(*The Thunder: Perfect Mind* 4:13)

We are here because of the sheer will and determination of our ancestors.

We are the daughters of Sojourner Truth who asked "Ain't I a woman??"

We are the daughters of Harriet Tubman who went back time and time again to free as many of the enslaved as she was able.

We are the daughters of Ella Baker who reminds us "We who believe in freedom cannot rest until it comes."

We are the daughters of Fannie Lou Hamer who endured physical abuse in jail, physical abuse attempting to register to vote, and medical abuse when she underwent what should have been a routine procedure and still sang "this little light of mine, I'm gonna let it shine."

We are the daughters of Claudette Colvin who knew her constitutional right and would not be moved.

We are the daughters of Maya Angelou who danced, and refused to turn away from passion, and called us Phenomenal.

We are the daughters of Alice Walker who showed us God in a field of purple.

We are the daughters of Toni Morrison who told us we had to love our flesh.

We are the daughters of Octavia Butler who wrote worlds past herself.

We are the daughters of Diahann Carroll who raised the bar and shifted the narrative for black women on television.

We are the daughters of Nichelle Nichols who helped us imagine ourselves in the future.

We are the daughters of Ruby Dee whose activism and art were synonymous.

We are the daughters of Billie Holiday who managed to get a song about the truth of lynching into the mainstream.

We are the daughters of Ella Fitzgerald who defined styles of music.

We are the daughters of Nina Simone who cursed the south's Jim Crow laws and practices in song.

We are the daughters of Aretha Franklin who taught us to be so serious about justice that we set aside a little bail money, just in case, in Jesus's name.

We are the daughters of Katherine Johnson who told us that if we liked what we did then we would do our best.

We are the daughters of Mary Jackson who took service as seriously as science.

We are the daughters of so many more not named here, who laid a path that we now follow.

We speak their names.

Papyrus fragment:
Apocryphon of John

THE ACTS OF
PAUL AND THECLA

Where discovered: Written sometime between late first century to mid-second century, there are St. Thecla churches all around the world, as there are for other saints.

When discovered: This text was never lost.

Length: A full and classic ancient novel of forty-five chapters in nine dense pages

Interesting fact: We can guess, based on the culture at the time, that Thecla probably would have been about fourteen years old at the beginning of this text and been of age to marry.

Where written: Based on its writing style, language, and references within the text, the closest approximation is that it was possibly written in what we now call Turkey.

ABOUT *THE ACTS OF PAUL AND THECLA*

This quite long epic features one of the most popular stories of a healer and teacher from the Jesus movements. Thecla was first a follower of the Apostle Paul. Through Paul, Thecla learned the teachings of Christ, essentially ghosted her fiancé, and left her home. She—like Paul—did not marry. Paul initially helped Thecla see the problems in traditional families and marriage. In Paul's First Letter to the Corinthians (1 Cor 7), Paul encouraged women and men to avoid marriage if possible, just as he did. Although Paul was not married, he did not forbid marriage nor did he encourage it. He said in this long biblical passage that "those who marry will have much trouble . . . and I wish you to be spared" (1 Corinthians 7:28b). But this *Acts of Paul and Thecla* tells stories that are more explicit about these troubles in marriage and the joys of living without marriage.

The story of Thecla and Paul from the first and second centuries is fascinating. Paul travels into town with two opportunity-seeking companions and stops at a fellow follower's home to rest. In the very first chapter, the hypocrisy of Paul's fellow travelers, Demas and Hermogenes, is made plain by our ancient author. Onesiphorus and his family have been waiting by the side of the road for Paul, whose reputation precedes him. Titus even gave a funny description of

Paul, so Onesiphorus knew what to look for. This is the only description of Paul that we have! Titus told Onesiphorus to keep an eye out for *"a man small in stature, with a bald head and crooked legs, healthy, with knitted eyebrows, a slightly long nose, and full of kindness—for at times he appeared as a human being and at others he had the face of an angel"* (3:2).

And when Paul saw Onesiphorus, he smiled and Onesiphorus said, "Welcome, servant of the blessed God!"

And Paul replied, "Grace to you and your household!"

But Demas and Hermogenes were jealous and went further into their hypocrisy so that Demos said, "Are we not of the Blessed, too, that you all have not welcomed us just as him?"

And Onesiphorus said, "I do not see in you the fruits of justice, but if you are anything, come to my house as well and rest." (4:1–3)

Hermogenes and Demos wanted to be greeted like Paul was greeted. The problem was, they were punching above their weight class. They hadn't put in the work; they didn't have Paul's experience to match their demands.

Onesiphorus let them know that their agenda was fully seen and understood. Still, he invited them to his home to rest. This moment in *The Acts of Paul and Thecla* is a valuable gift from early Jesus followers for use in social justice work. As the collective tries to uproot what is deeply entrenched, it is important to name the truths of a situation. How it is done determines whether it is a "calling out" or a "calling in." Onesiphorus in this text is an example of calling in. Onesiphorus essentially says: "You must earn your seat at the big table. I do not see where you've put in that work."

Thecla and Paul

Once at the home of Onesiphorus, Paul begins to teach. A young girl named Thecla overhears him through the window of her home and is transfixed. She sits at the window day and night, not moving even to eat or drink. Thecla's mother is troubled and sends for Thecla's fiancé, Thamyris. Despite his attempts, Thecla remains unmoved. Thamyris meets Paul's two ill-intentioned traveling buddies on the street. They devise a plan to have Paul answer to the governor. Paul is thrown in prison by the governor for teaching against marriage. Thecla is in trouble with the governor too for ignoring social law and her engagement to Thamyris, but she is not in prison. Both of them are under suspicion because Paul continues to warn women and younger people in general of the dangers in getting married and advocates for liberation and freedom instead. Thecla has become convinced by Paul's teaching about God and the dangers of getting married. Now to this small next story:

> *In the night Thecla took off her bracelets and gave them to the gatekeeper* (at her home, so that her mother would not know where she had gone), *and the door was opened to her.*

She went into the prison and gave the jailer a silver. She went into Paul and sat at his feet, and she heard the great things of God. And Paul feared nothing, having rights in the freedom of God, and Thecla strengthened her trust, kissing his chains. (18:1–2)

Thecla, a teenager, is running away from home to bribe her way into prison to visit Paul. Sitting at his feet in prison, she listens to the great things of God, especially those that relate to his program of living in new kinds of families. Paul is relaxed in prison; he feels free in prison. Thecla feels strong and full of trust. She kisses his chains, and although they continue to occasionally heal and teach together, there is no more intimacy in the story.

As a result of Thecla's trip to visit Paul in prison, the governor orders for Paul to be whipped and thrown out of the city. Thecla is also brought before the governor. Her mother cries out that Thecla should be burned so that all other women taught by Paul will be afraid. The governor is moved by this and condemns Thecla to burn. However, once Thecla climbs upon the pyre and a great fire is lit, it does not touch her.

And when she made the sign of the cross, she climbed upon the firewood. They lit it and a great fire blazed, but the fire did not touch her. For God, having compassion, caused a sound under the earth, and a cloud, filled with rain and hail, darkened the sky from above, and the vessel poured forth all that was in it. Many were in danger and died and the fire was extinguished. And Thecla was saved. (22:3b–4)

Thecla sets off to find Paul and when she does there is great rejoicing. Thecla says she'll cut her hair short (in the style of men) to be freer to heal and teach. Paul protests, saying she is too fair and, even though she had just survived a dangerous situation, tells her worse could come and she might not be as brave. She then says: *"Only give me the seal of Christ* (read: baptism) *and no trial will touch me"* (25:5). Paul tells her to "have patience" but never gets around to baptizing her.

Antioch

Another major part of the ancient story of the teenager Thecla is her encounter with Alexander, the Syrian Provincial Council President. Running away from Thecla's home town, the Apostle Paul and his young colleague Thecla headed for the large city of Antioch in Syria. Almost as soon as they got to Antioch, Alexander saw Thecla and fell in love with her. He approached Paul and offered him money and gifts for Thecla. But, Paul lied and said that he did not know Thecla at all, and said that Thecla did not "belong" to him.

So, since President Alexander was very powerful and Paul had denied knowing Thecla, the President embraced the young girl on the street. But she would have none of this and cried out intensely: *"Do not violate the stranger! Do not violate the slave of God! I am important among the Iconians and because I did not wish to marry Thamyris, I have been thrown out of the city"* (26:5b–6).

And she grabbed Alexander, ripped off his coat, and seized Alexander's crown from his head. This shamed him in public.

Alexander at once—still in love with her and also having been shamed by her—brought her to the governor. Thecla confessed what she had done, and the governor sentenced her to be killed by the wild beasts in the Arena.

Thecla was sent to the Arena and, though multiple attempts were made, she was not killed. One particular attempt is quite notable.

> *And they threw in many wild animals as she stood and stretched out her hands and prayed. But as she finished the prayer, she turned and saw a great pit full of water and said, "Now it is time for me to wash." And she threw herself in, saying, "In the name of Jesus Christ I baptize myself on the last day." And seeing this, the women and the whole crowd wept saying, "Do not throw yourself into the water!"; so that even the governor wept because the seals were going to devour such beauty. Then she threw herself into the water in the name of Jesus Christ, but the seals, seeing the light of a lightning flash, floated on the surface, dead. And surrounding her was a cloud of fire so that neither the wild animals could touch her nor could she be seen naked.* (34:1–6)

Thecla took seriously God's call on her life to teach and to heal. So seriously that she bucked the system that told her she had to be someone else, so seriously that when Paul didn't get around to baptizing her, she baptized herself. She took her own call to teach about Christ and to heal seriously enough to not let anyone else come before it, to not let Paul or anyone else come between her and God.

Thecla lived a long life as a healer and teacher. She was especially active with women and young people. She prompted them to break loose from families that, broken under the pressure of the Roman Empire, did not support young adult children and their wives and that had violent tendencies. She taught women and young adults how to become members of compassionate chosen families rather than father-driven families. She was able to help heal these younger adults and former wives of the brokenness and violence of traditional families.

Paul and Thecla did occasionally work together. Paul helped her learn how to become a healer and a teacher. However, in those significant times during which Paul was not with her, Thecla learned to trust more in herself and God for her ministry with women and young adults.

Paul's Message to Women and Youth

The Acts of Paul and Thecla sheds light on what the Apostle Paul thought about women and young people, which is not easy to understand when one reads the post-Pauline letters. There are two distinct pictures of how Paul treated women and youth, whether he encouraged them to be leaders and teachers or whether he stopped them from speaking and told them to follow men's teaching. New Testament readings are on both sides of this divide. The New Testament books Romans, I Corinthians, II Corinthians, Galatians, and the Acts of the Apostles read that Paul encouraged women and youth to lead and teach. Ephesians, Titus, I Timothy, and II Timothy represent Paul encouraging women and youth to be quiet and obey men leaders.

The Acts of Paul and Thecla is exciting because this very ancient and long book about Paul, women, and youth has a very clear picture of Paul teaching everywhere that women and young people should be free to teach. In this book, married men and government leaders are afraid of Paul's teaching and encouragement for women and youth. The governor and his soldiers throw Paul in jail for encouraging women and youth, and they try to kill Paul's woman cohort Thecla in the stadium.

> Family leaders and government leaders challenged Paul: *"All the women and youth go to* [Paul] *and are taught by him. . . . "* (9:1b). His opponents said: *"Bring him to the governor . . . on the charge of seducing the masses to the new teaching of the Christians. Then the governor will kill him* (Paul) *and you will have your wife. . . ."* (14:1, 2). Then the (betrothed men) went with the rulers, public officials, and a great crowd. . . . *"And Paul lifted up his voice . . . 'The living God . . . the self-sufficient God . . . has sent me so that I reclaim them from corruption . . . I bring good news . . . so that . . . humans have trust . . . of God and dignity . . .'"* (17:1, 2).

Following this, Thecla was again sentenced to death but was saved by God and a large crowd of women at the stadium. God, through nature, saves Thecla seven times throughout this story: a great storm (22:3–4), a ferocious lioness sits at her feet and then the same lioness saves Thecla from other animal attacks (33:1–5), a bolt of lightning (34:5), the women in the audience throw natural sedatives in with the wild animals (35:1–2a), fire frees her (35:4–5), and a huge rock saves her (44:2). She lived a full life as a teacher and healer, seeing Paul from time to time and being buried near him. *The Acts of Paul and Thecla* has been very popular reading for the past 1,800 years, and there are churches all over the world to St. Thecla. It is included in this book because, even with its popularity in some parts of the world, knowledge of this text and Thecla's empowering story is certainly not widespread.

Paul's Beatitudes

At the beginning of *The Acts of Paul and Thecla*, Paul shares his version of the beatitudes. Here are a few:

> *Blessed are the clear of heart for they will see God.*
> *Blessed are the self-possessed, for God will speak to them.*
> *Blessed are those who set themselves apart from this world, for they will please God.*
> *Blessed are those in awe of God, for they will become messengers of God.*
> *Blessed are the ones who tremble at God's words, for they will be called.*
> *Blessed are the ones who receive the wisdom of Jesus Christ, for they will be called children of the Highest.*
> *Blessed are the compassionate, for they will receive compassion and will not see the day of grievous judgment.* (5:1, 3, 4, 6; 6:1, 2, 6)

As you reflect on this ancient Christian text, consider our own beatitudes:

Blessed are those who pray.
Blessed are those who feel.
Blessed are those who keep trying.
Blessed are those who mess up.
Blessed are the open minded.
Blessed is she who resists.
Blessed are the fearful.
Blessed are those who don't conform.
Blessed are those who boldly stray.
Blessed are the wand'ring children.
Blessed are the unseen.
Blessed are the queer in spirit.
Blessed are you.
Blessed are you.
Blessed are you.

REFLECTIONS FOR TODAY ON *THE ACTS OF PAUL AND THECLA*

NEW FAMILY

William is twenty-seven years old, has a good job, and most days wakes up pretty happy. But this morning he awoke from a nightmare. It seemed like he had dreamt the whole night about his parents getting divorced. He knew that they had not divorced. He does feel that they should have. They are pretty old now, but they still yell at each other even after three decades of married life. And he knows there has been physical violence for much of their marriage.

This is not unlike many of his friends' families, but at least many of those marriages have been dissolved.

He does not like to think about his family. He has freed himself from those living nightmares and endless scenes of alcoholism.

But three things had happened over the last week that must have occasioned last night's nightmare: (1) he and his friend had argued fiercely for the first time since they moved in together; (2) William had seen his father walking alone on the street; and (3) he had read an ancient Christian story of a young woman called Thecla who had left her family and her fiancé for good, and instead lived with a group of people who acted like a loving family but had no bloodlines among them.

All three of these things now haunt him as he remembers the nightmare. That story written about the Apostle Paul and a young woman Thecla. It said the Apostle Paul was encouraging young people to live together in groups, to ask God for help in this new kind of family, and to be wary of the violence and raggedness of blood-related, father-driven families. He knew the real Bible did say that Paul did not get married but lived with similar groups as he traveled around teaching.

Some families love each other and care for each other, William knew, not all families are bad. He reminded himself of that this morning as he recovered from the nightmare. But what about Thecla and her new kind of family? Is that possible in this time, not just in Bible times?

> *Blessed are those who observe purity in the flesh, for they will become a temple of God. . . . Blessed are those who have wives as if they do not, for they will be heirs of God. . . . Blessed are the bodies of maidens, for they will have favor with God and will not lose the reward for their holiness; for the Father's word will be a work of salvation for them until the day of his Child, and they will have rest forever.*
>
> (*The Acts of Paul and Thecla* 5:2, 6; 6:7)

Thecla and Paul helped the people—especially the young people and the women—to live together in non-blood-related families. These pointed them successfully toward a strong communal life together that helped them avoid much cruelty that was inherent in both the marriages and blood families of that day. William in the twenty-first century has noticed that what Thecla and Paul did for so many first- and second-century young adults and single women of all ages is probably also needed for many twenty-first-century people.

THE PROTEST

In the height of summer Kenedy was out among others, pro-testing yet another killing of a Black person by police. They shouted out so many names—George Floyd, Sandra Bland, Breonna Taylor, Philando Castile—the list went on and on. This particular march took place on a long, hot day, but the crowd came prepared. One organization passed out small bottles of water to protesters, another had snack bags to share, a third passed out first-aid baggies and masks, and yet another group walked through the crowd with burning sage, blessing the space and cleansing energy as they passed. Various church groups marched together, praying and chanting. When one caller's voice got tired, another person led new calls. When one person got tired of carrying the banner, another person stepped in. It reminded Kenedy that she was enough to stand against systems of oppression and left her thinking: "What do I *already have* that I can contribute to the fight for justice?"

Like the women in this ancient text, Kenedy saw the protest-ers use whatever resources they had—be it their voices, sup-plies to share, strength to carry, scents to calm, prayers, and blessings.

In this passage of *The Acts of Paul and Thecla*, the women had proclaimed the governor's judgment to be evil and unholy. Then they used whatever they had at their disposal to aid in fighting such lawlessness.

And the women, when other, more frightening, wild animals were being thrown in, cried aloud, and some threw petals,

while others nard, and others cinnamon, and yet others car-
damom, so that there was an abundance of perfumes. And
all the wild animals which were let out were held as if by sleep
and did not touch her.

(*The Acts of Paul and Thecla* 35:1–2a)

Both then and now, people have used whatever is at their disposal to fight back against evil and the powers that uphold it.
Resistance always has been and always will be a communal
effort.

COMPASSIONATE CARE

"Can you take me to my doctor's appointment tomorrow?" Tess's mother asked her.

Tess picked up her mother the next day. Mama moved slowly as she got in the car. "Are you okay?" Tess asked.

"I'm not feeling so good," her mother replied.

"What's wrong?"

"I don't know."

Tess sighed. This had become a customary response.

The doctor's office was across town and took a long time to get to. She asked her mother: "Why do you go to this doctor? This is really far."

"Well," Mama said, "she wasn't that far before. She moved."

"You didn't want to change doctors?"

"I like her. She's nice."

Once they got there, Tess understood what Mama meant. The nurses in the office cheerfully greeted her mother as they took her vitals and confirmed her records. When the doctor entered the room, she greeted Mama with such joy and a warm embrace—holding her mother for a minute. The doctor was gentle and kind as she asked Mama how she was doing. She spoke in a loving tone and showed a mothering-like concern when Mama expressed discomfort and experienced pain. She rubbed Mama's back when Mama turned on her side in exhaustion. It stirred in Tess a renewed understanding of care. Sure this woman was caring for her mother, as was her job, but she also cared about Mama. Her compassion completely changed the energy in the space.

An ancient story in *The Acts of Paul and Thecla* tells of Queen Tryphaena who, even in her deep grief, showed tremendous compassion for a girl she didn't know. She took her in and not only cared for her, but cared about her.

And a rich queen, named Tryphaena, whose daughter had died, took Thecla into her care and found solace in her.
(*The Acts of Paul and Thecla* 27:4)

There are those in our sphere who need compassionate care. If it is you, may God present those to you who provide compassionate care. And may your compassionate heart meet the needs of others. May your loving acts be a source of fulfillment for you when you give what is needed when you seize the moment to do so.

TRUTH IS OUT

He pulled his coat closer around him, bracing against the cold wind. He still couldn't believe he was out. Out. Out on the streets of his old neighborhood with a house full of loved ones nearby. Out taking a walk, unsupervised. He glanced behind him to make sure. Out from behind barbed wire fences and prison bars. Out. He had been sentenced to life in prison without the possibility of parole. They wanted him to die there. But now, he was out. He tightly gripped a little scrap of paper where he'd scribbled down a couple of verses of beatitudes he'd found in a book in the prison library. He'd gone back to the library the day before he was released to jot them down. It was the only thing he'd wanted to take with him from that place.

> *Blessed are the self-possessed, for God will speak to them. Blessed are those who set themselves apart from this world, for they will please God.* (*The Acts of Paul and Thecla* 5:3–4)

He had it memorized by now but liked to keep it. He folded it back up into his wallet. These few verses had anchored him. They focused him and centered him through a really hard time. Through all those years. Through the many appeals. Through the countless hours spent poring over legal documents. Through the countless email exchanges between his legal team and the Innocence Project that sometimes swung like a pendulum between hope and despair. Through the tearful visits from his mama and his spouse. "You know who you are and WHOSE you are," his mama always said toward the end of their visits. Her faith in God was deep and had carried her through. She was much older now, moved slower, but she never gave up hope that he would be exonerated. He didn't really believe in God the same way she did, but he thought she might like these few lines. As he turned back and began to walk toward the family gathering to celebrate his return, he decided to share it with her later tonight.

THE MEAL

Cal loved to cook for his family. He was the keeper of all the family recipes—the ones from his granny, the ones his great-aunt shared with only him, even great-great-granddaddy's moonshine recipe. He'd memorized them all. Mac and cheese, corn casserole, rolls, yams, he made them all. He loved what cooking did to people. It brought them together around the table. It infused joy into the space. He pulled a handful of green beans from the bag and began to remove the ends, chuckling to himself about the time he brought a white friend home from college who ended up helping with food prep. When he had explained to her that they would be "picking beans," she thought they were going out into a field rather than just removing the stem that remained after you purchased them from the grocery store.

He moved about the kitchen with ease, checking boiling pots, peeking into the oven, washing greens, his playlist going in the background like a soundtrack to his work. Whatever the occasion, his family knew he would be delighted to prepare the meal. This particular meal was for the repast after his grandfather's Homegoing. Cal wanted each dish to be perfect. He'd found a book in his grandfather's belongings as he helped his mom sort through everything that came back from the nursing home. Flipping through the pages, he found the story of a girl who, despite what society wanted for her, had decided to live a different kind of life. He felt very much the same, having battled being gay in his Black conservative family. He was grateful that they had been open and willing to hear him, to shift in their understanding and continue to love him. Well, most of them anyway. He knew his grandfather had a strong hand in helping his family shift. Granddaddy had always insisted on love. His eyes caught a verse that read:

And there was much love in the tomb, Paul rejoicing, and Onesiphorus and all of them. And they had five loaves and vegetables and water and salt, and rejoiced at the divine works of Christ. (The Acts of Paul and Thecla 25:1–2)

There will be so much love and joy, he thought to himself, even in the midst of death. Granddaddy wouldn't want it any other way.

WIVES AND HUSBANDS

Thamyris, the man to be married to Thecla, has "more than a little anguish" because Thecla does not want to marry anyone. Thamyris says that he is "deprived of" his marriage. He says young men and young women are being *"deceived . . . that they should not marry, but remain as they are."* The crowd says, *"All of our wives have been seduced."*

Thecla says: *"Because I did not wish to marry Thamyris I have been thrown out of the city." I am indeed the slave of God . . . I have trusted in the Child of God, in whom God finds pleasure. . . . For God is a refuge for those in a storm, freedom for the oppressed, for the despairing a shelter. . ."* (*The Acts of Paul and Thecla* 11:2; 12:1; 13:3; 37:3, 4).

Husbands.

They sometimes bring coffee to their wives, while she sleeps in. They sometimes bring all the money in. They sometimes take care of the children.

They often watch a lot of football on television. Occasionally they mansplain. Sometimes they listen. Sometimes they beat women.

Sometimes they wash the dishes. Sometimes they are in charge of women. Occasionally they love women. Occasionally they love men.

When what it means to be a husband in the twenty-first century is examined carefully, it is clear that marriage, husbands, and wives are much less than a perfect institution. The mix of damage, love, and hurt in marriage is not about flaws in the married people themselves, any more than it is the inherent problems with the institution of marriage itself. Thecla's rejection of marriage in the comments above (*The Acts of Paul and Thecla* 11:2; 12:1; 13:3; 37:3, 4) carries important meaning for people in the twenty-first century, especially for women, men, genderfluid people, LGBTQIA2+, divorced, married, and those unsure of who they are relative to family and marriage. The freedom and love discovered by Thecla, Paul, and the many Jesus peoples who lived in communities of singles, couples, and complex family status can also be examples for twenty-first-century people today.

ENTERING THE ROCK

In a real gorge it is difficult to know which to be overwhelmed by the most. The roar of the water booms and bellows so that one cannot hear anything else. At the same time, the rocks through which the water runs press in on all sides, often forcing people into at least the spray of the water. Often the rock formations tower over the gorge so that one cannot even see the sky. And many of the looming rock configurations are so narrow and precipitous that one has to incline across the gorge for balance.

What these gorges feel like also takes on contrasting sensations. Often one simply feels as if the rock and the people have merged. But sometimes the slashing water and jaggedness of the facades engulf and overcome what is really happening. Many are thrilled by the mammoth power. Others feel comforted and held by nature itself. Frequently the beauty of the rock formations penetrates the humanity so much that people surrender and allow themselves to be surrounded by magnificence and immersed in energy.

This is a story about yet another time that the young woman Thecla in the first or second centuries was enthralled by the ways God kept giving her chances to grow and lead as well as frightened by the ways threatening men pushed her into danger. One time:

Greeks by religion and doctors by profession sent young men to her to ruin her. For they said, "she is a maiden and serves Artemis. Because of this, she has power with healing." And by

> *God's foresight she entered into a rock, alive and it descended*
> *under the earth* (*The Acts of Paul and Thecla* 44:1b).

In this story Thecla was saved by becoming part of the rock when the men were attempting to rape or kill her.

It is fascinating how Thecla's harrowing challenges and compelling gifts meet in the scary and beautiful gorges of nature. Her whole life is full of creative leadership in which women and young people come together in new kinds of family. At the same time, the violence of the Roman Empire is trying to maim, kill, or scare her without success.

Papyrus fragment:
Gospel of Philip

THE GOSPEL OF
MARY

Where discovered: One of several unknown and unnamed manuscript dealers had a large manuscript of *The Gospel of Mary* and other writings in the Upper Central Egyptian city of Achmim between 1875 and 1895. One of those manuscript dealers carried it to Cairo by 1896, but the first named person to purchase the cache of these manuscripts was German scholar Dr. Carl Reinhardt from one of the Egyptian Achmim scholars who had carried it to the Cairo markets. This papyrus manuscript has now been carbon-dated to the 400s.

When discovered: Between 1875 and 1895

Length: The largest manuscript of *The Gospel of Mary* is eighteen and one-quarter pages.

Interesting fact: Almost lost and almost destroyed in Germany during World Wars I and II, the first translation from the ancient Coptic language into German was published fifty-nine years after its purchase by Reinhardt in Egypt. It is now published in multiple languages and published in at least ten English versions. The most renowned and hailed translation and published book is by Professor Karen King at Harvard Divinity School.

ABOUT *THE GOSPEL OF MARY*

The Gospel of Mary is probably the most well-known of the relatively newly discovered ancient writings by the Jesus peoples
of the first and second centuries. This is the only gospel named
for a woman and she is the primary character in this gospel. In
this *Gospel of Mary* (it's not completely certain which ancient
Mary she is), Jesus is also a character in the book, and the
leader of a group of "disciples" (which means "students"). But
Mary is the most important character.

There's lots of action in this gospel, and Mary is usually at
or near the center of all action. Here we focus on perhaps the
biggest drama of this gospel. The story more or less begins
with Jesus finishing his time in the world. What follows here
is a summary of what happens in *The Gospel of Mary.* He has
already been killed by the Roman rulers and he comes back
for a last post-death appearance with his students. He reminds
them of key parts of his teaching: *"Peace! The Child of Humanity is with you all. Follow it. Those who seek it will find it. Do not
lay down any rules, lest you be confined by them"* (4:5, 10).

Then Jesus leaves them for good.

Immediately these followers and students of Jesus weep and
panic, saying: *"How shall we proclaim the good news? If they did
not spare him, how will they spare us?"* (5:2).

Then Mary stands up, encouraging them not to be afraid:
"His grace will be with you and shelter you. He has prepared us

and made us humans." The Gospel of Mary then says that *"when Mary said this, she turned their hearts to the Good"* (5:6, 9).

What an extraordinary development! The disciples fall apart as Jesus leaves them, but Mary rescues them. This recovered gospel shows her as the key leader of the new movement. It is the only gospel of ancient Jesus followers that has a woman as its primary character and very probably refers to Mary Magdalene (although there were many women named Mary in the Israel of that time).

The Gospel of Mary was written about the same time as the Gospel of Luke in the Bible, probably around 120 CE. This ancient text portrays Mary Magdalene in relationship to male authorities of the first two centuries of Jesus people.

Peter said to Mary, "Sister, we know that the Savior loved you more than the rest of women. Tell us the words of the Savior which you remember . . . and we do not. . . ." (6:1–2a)

"I," she said, "I saw the Lord in a vision" . . . Mary then told them of the vision from the Savior Jesus she had seen. After Mary (told them the vision) *she was silent, since it was to this point that the Savior had spoken with her. (7:3 . . . 9:29)*

But Andrew responded and said to the brothers and sisters, "Say what you will about what she has said, I do not believe that the Savior said this, for certainly these teachings are strange ideas." Peter responded and spoke concerning these same things. He questioned them about the Savior, "Did he really speak with a woman without our knowing about it? Are we to turn around and listen to her? Did he choose her over us?"

Then Mary wept and said to Peter, "My brother, Peter, what are you thinking? Do you think that I have thought this up myself in my heart, or that I am telling lies about the Savior?"

Levi then responded and said to Peter, "Peter, you have always been an angry person. Now I see you contending against the woman like the adversaries. But if the Savior made her worthy, who are you, then, to reject her? Surely the Savior's knowledge of her is trustworthy. That is why he loved her more than us. Rather, let us be ashamed. We should clothe ourselves with the perfect Human, acquire it for ourselves as he commanded us, and proclaim the good news, not laying down any other rules or other laws beyond what the Savior said."

After he (Levi) had said these things, they started going out to teach and proclaim. (10:1–14)

Although throughout much of Christianity Mary Magdalene is often portrayed as a repentant prostitute, the idea that Mary Magdalene was a repentant prostitute is not found in the Bible at all. The idea about Mary as a repentant prostitute did not occur until Pope Gregory said this in a sermon in 591, hundreds of years after the New Testament came into existence.

The Gospel of Mary—written almost 500 years before Pope Gregory—also has nothing at all about Mary as a prostitute.

The Gospel of Mary shows Mary's leadership. She is the key leader who revived the disciples, just as she can empower people as they face their work for social justice and as they "make us true Human beings" (5:8). As author Karen King summarizes, Mary Magdalene is "the first woman apostle."[1]

---

[1] Karen King, *The Gospel of Mary of Magdala: Jesus and the First Woman Apostle* (Polebridge Press, 2003), vi.

REFLECTIONS FOR TODAY
ON *THE GOSPEL OF MARY*

"LET IT SHINE"

"This little light of mine," she sang along with the choir, "I'm gonna let it shine."

It was Children's Sunday at church. And this was their big song. They had been practicing for weeks. Jess had earned a big solo verse and she'd been practicing extra hard all week long in preparation.

"Let it shine, let it shine, let it shine! All in my home, I'm gonna let it shine. . . ."

Her mama had taken her on a trip to the beauty salon yesterday for a special hairdo instead of having Auntie CeeCee come over with her hot comb. Mama said she could choose whatever style she wanted. But when mama returned to pick her up and saw the faux hawk with her curls and kinks loose and the two braids dandling past her ears with beads at the bottom, the color drained from her face. "If that's what you wanted, Jessye," her mama said. Her mama was a fierce lover of opera so she never abbreviated Jess's name like her friends did. She knew her mama wanted her to get something "more appropriate for church" but Jess didn't care. She thought this hairstyle made her look more grown up. She couldn't wait to try on her new dress with her ruffled socks and patent leather shoes. All the other girls her age were wearing pantyhose but mama said twelve was too young and she'd have to wait until she was in high school.

"Let it shine, let it shine, let it shine!"

It was time for her big solo! "God gave it to me, I'm gonna let it shine" she sang, throwing in a couple of extra notes and changing the melody slightly like she'd practiced over the week. "Yes, Lawd, let him use you!" she heard from the Amen corner.

As they drove to church this morning, Jess was nervous. She was absent-mindedly going over the verse in her head while mama listened to the preacher on the radio. She heard him say,

> *Beware that no one lead you astray saying "Look over here!" Or "Look over there!" For the Child of Humanity is within you! Follow it! Those who seek it will find it. Then go and proclaim the good news of the realm.*
>
> (*The Gospel of Mary* 4:3–8)

She felt like that preacher was speaking just to her. She knew that this morning, God was within her and she was proclaiming the good news through song.

"Let it shine, let it shine, let it shine!"

As she finished the congregation applauded. You could hardly hear the group of little ones in front of her singing "Hide it under a bushel—NO! I'm gonna let it shine!" She smiled, knowing she'd done her best to praise God on this special day.

MARY'S ALLY

Early in her ministry, Pam was sometimes left out of learning experiences. The men were always asked first and it was hard for her to get a chance to practice. Men always received credit for collective work. Men were invited into more opportunities. Though they all saw it and recognized it for what it was, there was not a "Levi" as depicted in this ancient Christian text.

> *Peter said to Mary, "Sister, we know that the Savior loved you more than the rest of the women. Tell us the words of the Savior which you remember, which you know and we do not, nor have we heard them." Mary answered and said, "What is hidden from you I will tell you." (The Gospel of Mary 6:1–3)*

So then Mary proceeds to share with them, over the span of several chapters, her vision she had of the Savior. When she finished, she was silent.

> *But Andrew responded and said to the brothers and sisters, "Say what you will about what she has said, I do not believe that the Savior said this, for certainly these teachings are strange ideas." Peter responded and spoke concerning these same things. He questioned them about the Savior, "Did he really speak with a woman without our knowing about it? Are we to turn around and all listen to her? Did he choose her over us?"*

> *Then Mary began to weep and said to Peter, "My brother, Peter, what are you thinking? Do you think I have thought*

this up myself in my heart, or that I am telling lies about the Savior?" Levi responded and said to Peter, "Peter, you have always been an angry person. Now I see you contending against the woman like the adversaries. But if the Savior made her worthy, who are you, then, to reject her?"

(The Gospel of Mary 10:1–9)

By this point in our ancient context, the resurrection story had circulated, complete with the part where the women find the empty tomb. Written probably around the same time as the Gospel of Luke, it tracks with the narrative of that gospel where the women tell the eleven apostles and also aren't believed. In fact, it's Peter who gets up and runs to the tomb to check for himself.

An important lesson to glean from Mary's experience is for women to find men like Levi, in fact, surround themselves with Levis. And for men to be Levis instead of Peters.

As Pam moved on in ministry, she found some Levis—men who recommended her, saying when opportunities arose: "I know the perfect person for this; she's been working on this for a while" and who told her: "I think you're the right person to do this work with me," or "Your voice needs to be in this room; I'm bringing you in."

With these Levis, she didn't have to ask or push. She got to do her work to the best of her ability and moved according to its merits. Levis are focused on creating the world they wish to see—one that is more equal, one where everyone is valued— and in dismantling and disrupting systems that stand in the way.

SHE TURNED THEIR HEART TO THE GOOD

The Gospel of Mary 5:6, 9 reads "Mary Magdalene turned their heart to the Good."

What that means today is what happens inside people as their hearts turn toward the Good:

The young woman who has lost hope feels the kindness of calls in this moment of loss and desire.

Three friends visit a neighbor who fell down the stairs.

Siblings looked at each other and roared with anger when they heard news of another shooting in a supermarket.

The whole crowd broke into laughter at the potty joke.

His boyfriend reappeared after two weeks of silence.

The whole city felt the surprise and power of their first official Juneteenth.

Listening to Mahatma Gandhi turned the heart of India to the Good.

Almost everyone in the school took to the street to protest.

She could feel how much Goodness mattered after so many months of mix-ups and loneliness.

The Blessed One said . . . , Peace be with you. Bear my peace within yourselves . . . For the Child of Humanity is within you. Follow it. (The Gospel of Mary 4:1–3, 5)

Papyrus fragment:
The Gospel of Truth

THE GOSPEL OF
TRUTH

Where discovered: *The Gospel of Truth* was a part of the very famous fifty-one manuscripts found in the stone jar in the middle of the Egyptian Desert in 1945.

When discovered: 1945

Length: Twenty-six chapters that turn out to be eight pages of twenty-first-century English.

Interesting fact: The first guesses as to who wrote *The Gospel of Truth* focused on the word "gnosticism," a modern word for "heresy" that did not even exist for the first 1,600 years of Christianity. Now, after some seventy years of reading this gospel, "gnosticism" is making less sense to all kinds of readers. These days, there is much more interest in this gospel, but there is no real breakthrough in identifying a likely author.

When written: When *The Gospel of Truth* was written is one of the more difficult questions; it is probably best to just say sometime in the second century.

ABOUT *THE GOSPEL OF TRUTH*

The Gospel of Truth is not a story like the New Testament Gospel of Mark or the ancient Jesus peoples' writing *The Gospel of Mary*. Nor is it a long list of teachings of Jesus like *The Gospel of Thomas*, one of the most popular newly discovered ancient writings of Jesus followers. Rather, it sounds by turns like a poem, a letter, or a feeling-filled sermon:

> *The Father is sweet and within his desire is goodness. . . . The Father's children are his fragrance for they are from the beauty of his face. Because of this, the Father loves his fragrance and discloses it everywhere, and when it mixes with matter it gives his fragrance to the light.* (19:1, 4–5)

The Gospel of Truth's most powerful and sensuous dimensions are how goodness and beauty continue to overflow everywhere. This gospel lays out one of the most elegant descriptions of humanity:

> *Say then from the heart that you are the perfect day and within you dwells the light that never ends. Speak of the truth with those who seek it and of knowledge with those who have sinned through their transgression. Strengthen the feet of those who stumble and stretch your hand to those who are*

weak. Feed those who are hungry and give rest to the weary. (17:11–14)

This passage is a reminder that God has made people strong and good. This ancient cousin to the Bible reiterates what the first book of the Bible has God saying so clearly—announcing (seven times) how good humanity is and all the universe is good. *The Gospel of Truth* was written somewhere in the second century. The tenderness of the writing is matched by its sense of human power and understanding:

Raise those who wish to arise and awaken those who sleep— for you are all understanding drawn forth. If strength does these things, strength becomes stronger. (17:16, 17)

It helps us to understand the freshness of this writing by noticing what the title of the book means. The word that is translated into English as "gospel" misses much of its meaning—this particular "Gospel" presses the basic meaning of "Gospel" as "Good News." This *Gospel of Truth* underlines more directly specific goodness at the intersection of what it means to be human in hard times.

It seems to have been written for and by people who have had one or many painful things happen to them. Thousands of the Jesus people were tortured, enslaved, and thrown out of countries by the Roman Empire. But these people then made a stunning reversal and reclaimed a vibrant life.

This nine-page document knows the experiences of *"confusion, instability, fear, divisions, many illusions, disturbing dreams, being beaten, people trying to kill them, torture and torment"* (14:11–13; 16:8). But despite this level of disaster, shock, and failure, the main message is in its first sentence: *"The true good news is joy!"* Even while there is consciousness of pain and loss, this book is lush in its description of what has happened to all of those who have come back from having fallen apart, having lost their love, and having had their life broken in pieces.

For those who have discovered this ancient writing in our twenty-first century, most cling tightly to *The Gospel of Truth*'s description of how one's own rebirth turns out to change the bigger world:

> *This is the good news of the one whom they seek, related to those filled through the mercies of God . . . Jesus Christ shone to the one in the darkness of forgetfulness. He enlightened them and showed them a way. . . . He discovered them in himself, and they discover him in themselves. . . . All things are in him and all things have need of him. . . . Everything was in need of him, like someone who is not known but desires to be known and loved. . . . He became a guide, at rest and at leisure. He came into their midst and spoke a teacher's words in places of learning.* (4:1–3, 7, 8; 5:6, 8)

When people experience God in most cultures, it seems to come most commonly in several ways: sight, sound, dreams, and perhaps to a lesser extent touch. In many cases, particular persons lean toward one or two of these events more than other people. Hearing the roar of the sea? Or seeing sunrise or sunset? Or dreaming an impossible sight or sound? Or maybe sometimes being touched so that one's whole body is alive?

All of these experiences of depth and/or God tend to be intensely beautiful, full of longing, and/or penetrating as feelings. Words like "blessing," "overwhelming," "miraculous," "awe-inspiring," or "hallowing" can be ways of characterizing such moments. And for most, such experiences—whether one believes in God or not—are full of thankfulness; they are life-changing incidents and sometimes at the same time overpowering sensations.

The Gospel of Truth is some of the most sensuous religious reading one can find. Its sumptuous vocabulary contains fullness, mercies, fruit, desires, passionate, bounty, body, embrace, sweetness, dreams, beloved, flesh, heart, awaken, warm, trust, ointment, create, secret, within, kisses, fresh, flows, and loves.

This sensuousness points to another holder of experience of divinity and depth. For *The Gospel of Truth,* there is yet a sense that holds God and deepness more than any other. This is the sensuousness of fragrance, and how it makes the experience of God and deepness real as we saw previously in 19:5, 6: *"God loves God's fragrance and discloses fragrance everywhere . . . when fragrance mixes with matter, it gives fragrance to the light . . . God makes fragrance that surpasses every form and every sound . . ."*

Artist John Quick studied the way fragrance made people remember experiences from their past. He brought some ninety different fragrances to patients in Boston hospitals and demonstrated how simply these individual scents in their hospital rooms brought dozens of experiences from their past forward. It is quite easy for people today to do this in any part of their life. Just holding a particular fragrance to one's nose often brings forth powerful and deep experiences from one's past and present. A strawberry, a glass of water from a stream, any kind of perfume, most flowers, a hamburger fresh off the grill, or a crayon prompts long-ago friends and family, places, hopes, challenges, and loves.

This profound meaning and spirituality is unfortunately not a common experience for people in much of our American cultures and is especially rare in Protestant Christianity. *The Gospel of Truth*'s devotion to the profuse dimension of God and life itself could easily match and surpass one's favorite stories, mementos, and lovers. And it is quite clear that fragrances are primary ways to bring powerful and hidden experiences quickly to the surface in Hindu, Buddhist, Orthodox, Native, and traditional Catholic festivals and temples. God-like and other deep experiences are tied directly to unexpected and breath-taking hidden moments in our lives. Here's to the possibilities that such deep, God-centered habits, practices, and rituals can reappear fragrantly in peoples' encounters, just as in the reading of *The Gospel of Truth*.

As *The Gospel of Truth* honors creation, the place humans have in it, the hugeness of everything, the harmony and diversity of it all, it wraps it in one of the most sensuous of dedications.

Receiving the face of all things, and purifying them, bringing them back to the Father, the Mother, Jesus of boundless sweetness. (10:6)

Here the sensuousness and holiness of life, spirit, nature, relationships, and God is laid alongside this dedication from *The Gospel of Truth*. It unfolds slowly, letting it unfold in terms of the human body, merging such experience with the all, and permeating a larger sensuousness that is at the heart of this cousin of the Bible.

Receiving the face of all things

The oldest continent of humankind, Africa held humankind since approximately 1.9 million years ago in multiple forms, with all kinds of fascinating developments of diverse minds and cultures

Micro-organisms in hydrothermal vents since about 3.4 billion years

The universe exploding into existence fifteen billion years ago, still expanding out in all directions

The birth of jazz in the early nineteenth century

The colors of the northern lights

Purifying them

As the galaxies and human families continue to elaborate, all of it is refining and distilling an ensemble of realities and beauties

Fire, water, earth, and air purify the world against pollutants

Bringing them back to the Father

Father is sweet and within his desire is goodness (19:1)
In which we might find rest (19:2)
Loving his fragrance from the beauty of all faces (19:4)

The Mother,

Unlike most trinities, this dedication has the Mother at the very center of divinity's power and aliveness (10:6)
All stretch toward the full one alone, who is a Mother for them (27:2)

Jesus of boundless sweetness

Fascinating is the final phrase in this benediction of The Gospel of Truth, which ties the Mother to Jesus of boundless sweetness. It is not clear whether Jesus is the Mother of boundless sweetness, or whether Jesus of boundless sweetness is the third part of the dedication's "trinity" of *To the Father, to the Mother, Jesus of boundless sweetness.*

The picture of the Father in this gospel is so gentle, even describing him as sweet. It is not the picture of the Almighty God painted in contemporary Christianity, not so much conquest, power, or aggression. As the title of this writing says, Good News!

Here one finds large-scale reframing of God in relation to breath and spirit. How might knowing this change how people interact with each other? What weight does that remove from their shoulders? If people remember that it is not about the words they say, but rather the presence they bring into each room, the fragrance of the Divine is juicy and verdant.

This gives the phrase "putting on airs" a different look. It's commonly used to describe someone who acts as though they think they're better than everyone else. But according to *The Gospel of Truth*, the "airs" of the "fragrance of God's Children" emit love, compassion, empathy, and purpose. They mix with the energy, or "matter" as the passage reads, and serve to lift the spirits. The divine co-mingles with itself, breathing in, immersing, and allows people to move even just a hair closer in their call to goodness in this world. It is a sweet sweet spirit in each place that is the spirit of the Lord.

The Gospel of Truth rejects that the problem is sin or that humanity is inherently sinful. This now recovered gospel says the problem is simply *"the darkness of forgetfulness."* No repentance is necessary. In fact, there is *"good news . . . revealed through mercies . . ."* All one needs is to remember people's connectedness.

The Gospel of Truth goes even further in laying out how available connections between people are. This good news is "in the midst" of people. All one has to do is remember or look and see "a way." That is, people do not need to see the way, but just any way (4:7; 5:8–12). Or as *The Gospel of Thomas* also says: *"The realm of God is spread out upon the earth, but people don't see it"* (113:3).

Even more to the point about how humanity—big and small—can "remember" and dispel the darkness of forgetfulness, *The Gospel of Truth* shows an inherent process that allows people to recollect, see, and access their connections to one another. It is simply a matter of being alongside the presence "at rest" and "at leisure."

This gospel outlines explicitly how simply the presence naturally opens to all people their active awareness of their greater connectedness. In other words, there is no secret code and no special knowledge. This innate process can start with people or can start with Jesus. In any case, the unconnected sense of alienated people simply disappears in the simple presence of people and/or Jesus Christ. They both effortlessly prompt one another's presence, and the alienation is forgotten.

REFLECTIONS FOR TODAY
ON *THE GOSPEL OF TRUTH*

COUGH . . . COUGH!

Taylor met up with a friend who was in town for a short visit. As they waited for a light to change, a man nearby coughed. Productively. In the time of COVID-19. Sans mask. Without covering his mouth. Near her germaphobic self. (Did she mention he was nearby??) She looked in his direction and said: "Oh no, I don't like that." She noticed the man look up at them as they moved away.

The light changed and the two women crossed the street as they continued their conversation. A minute later, they heard the same productive cough nearby. "Oh no, I don't like that," she said again as she glanced back and saw the man dart away. That feeling came over her that women get when they know a man is targeting them—be it unwanted sexual advances or to prove to themselves the insignificance of womankind. It is always, at minimum, annoying and, at worst, scary. In this situation, a white man simply didn't like the way a Black woman looked at him with disapproval and wanted to get under her skin.

She had to admit, it did. She was annoyed. She was grossed out. Taylor said to her friend: "He did that on purpose!"

"Yep, he did," her friend replied.

In the whole scheme of life, it was an insignificant act that was intended to assert power over them. But they released it immediately and went on with their time together.

> *Now their works lie scattered, but in time oneness will make the places full. In oneness all will return to themselves, within knowledge purifying themselves from multiplicity into oneness, devouring matter within themselves like fire, and darkness by light, death by life. If indeed these things have happened to each one of us, it is necessary for us to think about all things so that this house might be holy and tranquil in oneness.* (*The Gospel of Truth* 11:1–3)

Most marginalized people reading this can automatically think of a time (or several) when a microaggression was directed toward them. In those moments, it can feel comforting to have someone acknowledge and validate the experience, no matter how small. That acknowledgment creates a sense of unity, a bond in holy and tranquil oneness.

ENNUI

Jax stared absently out the window. He was in year three of working remotely, which he had initially loved until it turned, within three months, into work-from-home. He relied heavily on variety in his schedule to keep his mild ADHD in check. He planned trips all over the world in resorts with great Wi-Fi and immersed himself in different cultures. He felt an alignment in his identity with each new place. He meticulously planned every detail, every time change. His calendar was full of the multiple colors of good organization skills. But now, with travel almost completely removed, his days had become monotonous and he was having more and more trouble staying focused. His job had become tedious. The beginnings of various projects and hobbies littered the surfaces of his apartment as well as his computer's desktop.

Alone in his tiny apartment, Jax felt the tinges of depression and anxiety color the edges of everything. "How much longer," he thought, "will I have to live like this?"

Grabbing his mask he went out to check the mail. There was no one in the hallway. He imagined most people in this small complex had left, except for the clumsy kangaroo with bowling balls and an expensive sound system that seemed to live above him.

He sifted through his mail once he got back in his apartment and found a card his sister had sent him. He opened it. The front of the card read,

Now their works lie scattered, but in time oneness will make the places full. In oneness all will return to themselves, within knowledge purifying themselves from multiplicity into oneness, devouring matter within themselves like fire, and darkness by light, death by life. If indeed these things have happened to each one of us, it is necessary for us to think about all things so that this house might be holy and tranquil in oneness. (*The Gospel of Truth* 11:1–3)

"I know this has been a difficult time for you," Fe wrote inside. "Hoping you are able to find yourself in the middle of all this. Think of this season as a return to yourself."

He picked up the phone immediately and called her up. "I got your card," he said dryly when she answered.

"Well hello to you, too!" she countered, amused.

"I'm sorry," he said. "It's just . . . literally what am I supposed to do? What actual steps do I take? This is getting old."

"Have you tried meditation?" she asked. "I can send you some resources to explore. We can even practice together, if you want. Obviously it won't fix everything, but you may find that centering yourself, bringing everything back to the core, finding oneness within yourself may help give you a daily purpose and long-term goal in a time when everything feels scattered. I started practicing every day and it has really helped."

He sighed. He was more continental backpacking and nightclubs than yoga and meditation retreats, but he was desperate for a little respite from this brain fog that seemed to have settled in. "Sure, whatever," he said. "I'm in."

"Great!" Fe gushed, a little too excitedly for his taste. "I'll email you some stuff now!"

He hung up and flipped the card back over to the front, read it again, and secretly hoped that holy and tranquil oneness was possible for him.

This passage from *The Gospel of Truth* speaks of a divided nature and what is necessary to come back together. The answer isn't as far off as it may seem. This oneness comes from within.

ARE YOU SLEEPING?

Most of Ellis's life was a search for knowledge. Knowing things and being smart was valued in his family. No, he didn't get the highest grades, he wasn't valedictorian, he didn't win scholarships, but the act of learning, of figuring things out, was highly regarded. This, however, was an outward pursuit for a good portion of his life. It wasn't until later that his entire paradigm shifted from knowledge to awareness. It was as if Ellis had been awakened to a whole new way of being and a whole new way of thinking. It was a slow awakening, as being awakened by the sunrise. Sleep hangs on the edges as one becomes more and more aware of the light. Even today, he feels as if he is still awakening. And as he becomes a little more awake, it shifts the way he operates in the world. The Spirit rights him, once again, setting him on his feet.

Such are those who cast ignorance from themselves like sleep. They do not consider it anything or its works as real things, but leave them behind like a dream in the night. Knowledge of the Father they value as the dawn. Each one acted as if asleep when he was without knowledge. And this is the way he comes to knowledge—as if awakened. Good for the one who returns to one's self and awakens. . . . And when this one awakened, the Spirit pursued in haste. Having given its hand to those spread on the ground, it set them on their feet—for they had not yet arisen. (The Gospel of Truth 15:1–9)

Oprah Winfrey says: "When you know better, you do better." Ellis went into seminary thinking he knew how it all worked only to have all that he knew exploded. He came out, however, with a fuller awareness in which to root all that he learned. All those exploded pieces came together again, but in different ways. The relationship that he had with God when he went into seminary and the relationship he had with Her when he came out were vastly different and he wouldn't trade that for anything in the world.

His current prayer is that where he once thought it was more important to be knowledgeable, he now looks to be aware; where he once thought it paramount to show how smart he was, he now reads the room to see what's needed; and where he once contributed to upholding the system of white supremacy, he now uproots it at every opportunity he can find. May it be so.

Papyrus fragment:
Faiyum Papyri

THE THOUGHT OF
NOREA

Where discovered: *Norea* was found in the jar now referred to as the Nag Hammadi Library.

When discovered: Like *The Gospel of Thomas, The Thunder: Perfect Mind, The Gospel of Truth*, and some forty-eight other Jesus peoples' writings, *Norea* was discovered in 1945.

Length: Two-and-a-third papyrus pieces of paper in 50 lines

Interesting fact: This writing is a song or poem that praises a divine female connected deeply to the Father of All. She has the great mind of the Invisible One and she "has four holy helpers who intercede with the Father of All." She is also the daughter of Eve and Adam, and rescued Eve from the violent rulers of the world.

ABOUT *THE THOUGHT OF NOREA*

One of the most recent discoveries of Jesus people writings of the first two centuries has come through the fascinating "Jesus Jar" in the middle of the Egyptian desert. A fairly large jar was found in 1945 by two farmers. Inside the jar were fifty-one different writings in the ancient Coptic language, almost all of which had something to do with Jesus. More than half of these parchments had not been seen before. It is thought that this jar had been taken, perhaps hidden, from a nearby monastery. The collection, now all at the Coptic Museum in Cairo, has been named The Nag Hammadi Library, named after the small town near where the jar was found. The first full English publication of these fifty-one writings was released in 1979.

One of the last of the Nag Hammadi texts to be studied is *The Thought of Norea*. Very little of *Norea* has been studied until recently. An important study is in Celene Lillie's newly heralded Fortress Press publication called *The Rape of Eve*. A similar set of studies is now also available at the website "Early Christian Texts" (earlychristiantexts.com).

Norea is an overlapping ancient character, known both as the daughter of Eve and a Savior from above. As Eve's daughter, she is becoming known as a powerful figure who was able to fight against the evil rulers of the world when they attacked

Eve herself. Very similar—but not exactly the same—Norea was a Savior from God who fought successfully against the Roman Empire, not unlike Jesus in The Revelation to John and the Secret Revelation of John.

How many divine characters enter the world on behalf of God's love and rescue in the Bible and beyond! In the Bible, Wisdom herself and the Son of Man (sometimes translated as "the Child of Humanity") come to earth to create and rescue people. In other writings of Israel and the early Jesus peoples Wisdom, the Son of Man/Child of Humanity, Seth, Norea, Adam, Eve, Jesus, and Paul save and rescue people and groups.

The story of Eve and Adam has them give birth to Cain and Abel who then brought the disaster of murder to humankind. The biblical story of Eve and Adam continues then in their love for each other to bring forth a third son, Seth, named in several places in the Bible in the line of Eve and Adam's line of humanity. As powerful and loving daughter and powerful and faithful son of Eve and Adam, Norea and Seth were saviors of future humanity, alongside Jesus.

"It was Norea who cries out to Light dwelling in the heights, Voice of Truth, and upright Word." (27:20–22).

The Truth's voice, Light and the Word *"received Norea into her place forever." They gave Norea the Father of All so that she might inherit the first mind and "might rest in the divine self-generation." She creates herself and she "inherits*

*the living Word." "She speaks with the mind of the Father.
And she began to speak with the words of Life." (28:12, 13)*

What a powerful and life-giving person! In many ways she is very much like Jesus, both profoundly human and definitely divine. Just as Jesus in the Bible cries out to God, "Why have you abandoned me?"(Mark 15:34); Norea begs for the Light, Truth, and Word. Both Jesus and Norea are Saviors for many humans, and both live with God. *The Thought of Norea* says *"there will be days when she will see the Fullness"* and *"holy helpers will intercede on her behalf with the Father of All,"* (28:20–29) not unlike the Father interceding for Jesus in the Gospel of John (John 17). Both of the latter children of Eve and Adam (Seth and Norea) also live on (like Jesus) to save many people, especially against the evil rulers of Rome.

The extracanonical book *The Thought of Norea* recounts a new kind of divine power that Norea has. Norea, who sometimes is divine, has the ability to generate herself. Or, as *The Thought of Norea* says, she lives in "the Divine Autogenes." This Greek word ("autogenes") is best translated as "God's Self-Generator."

Here and in other reflections, Norea stands up for people in trouble and rescues them.

REFLECTIONS FOR TODAY
ON *THE THOUGHT OF NOREA*

IS NOREA STILL HELPING PEOPLE TODAY?

Laney and Jim are a comical duo. There is hardly any furniture in Jim's two-bedroom house. The upstairs bedroom has a bed in it. There is a small refrigerator, a two-burner stove, and a barebones sink. He is seventy-two years old and has been completely blind for the last thirty years. Laney's job is to visit Jim two times a week, and she has been doing that for eight years. She herself is poor, but not like Jim. She smiles so much when she thinks of Jim. It does make her feel not so poor, and she laughs out loud every two weeks when she brings in his braille *Playboy* magazine. Sometimes he reads it to her. She has seen his son twice in the eight years. And a good fifteen times she has found Jim at the bottom of his stairs after he had fallen. That always shakes her.

Not unlike the powerful ancient spiritual leader Norea, Laney keeps Jim alive and connected to the bigger world. But just like Norea, Elisha, and a number of angels have divine power, Laney can not always make everything perfect for Jim in his blindness and poverty.

"It was Norea who cries out to Light dwelling in the heights, Voice of Truth, and upright Word" (The Thought of Norea 27:20–22). They continued to attack her, but God sent the angel Eleleth to come to Norea's aid. There were times in her

life that Laney too had been accosted. And Laney's courage and strength sometimes save Jim. It is probably the case that how she has rescued Jim many times really comes in great part from the times she has had to save herself from poverty and beatings. She worries for Jim's safety when he is alone, especially in those cases when someone breaks in. She has found evidence that in lighting the stove he would have small fires in the kitchen. Whether Laney is like Norea or Eleleth is a close call.

MARCH FOR OUR LIVES: WHEN CRYING OUT IS SALVIFIC

Billie met Mira for brunch before they headed to the March for Our Lives rally organized to address the rampant gun violence in the United States following a series of mass shootings that included children at an elementary school in Uvalde, Texas. Mira had just interviewed for an opening at Billie's workplace earlier that week and, during that time, they realized that they were both attending the rally alone. They decided to meet up and go together.

Before the march, they met for brunch where they got better acquainted, discovered different connections they shared in their work and with people in ministry, and dug into ministerial musings. By the time they walked over to the Washington Monument, they had built a warm sense of connection.

As they arrived, they discussed an exit strategy. They both had their fair share of rally, march, and protest experience but Billie's boss had impressed upon her the importance of a safety plan, just in case. "Okay," Billie said to Mira, "if something should happen, we will head out that way or straight back whichever is safest. And no matter what, we will not leave each other." They picked a spot in the second section back, so they weren't crowded in or close to the stage.

A little over an hour into the rally, the organizers asked for a moment of silence. During that moment of silence, someone was shouting out in the distance near the stage area. The moment of silence ended and suddenly everyone began to run toward the direction of Mira and Billie. They turned and ran as well from the unknown threat and potential trampling. Billie looked over as she ran and saw that Mira was not with her; she had tripped and fallen over another person. Billie turned around and went back for her, helping her up off the ground. "This way!" They held hands and ran in the direction of their first exit plan. They made it about fifty feet before an older Black woman with a gray Afro spoke into the microphone, "Freeze! Stop running. There is no issue here."

Everyone stopped running.

"We will continue on. We will not let this take our focus."

Mira burst into tears. "That was terrifying! I'm so glad I didn't bring my kids."

Billie was filled with rage as she felt her own tears brim. "It is absolutely ridiculous that we live like this."

Enough is enough.

It is Norea who cries out to them. They heard, [and] they received her into her place forever. . . . And she began to speak with the words of Life, and [she] remained in the presence of the Exalted One, possessing that which she had received before the world came into being. (The Thought of Norea 27:20; 28:12–17)

Later, Mira and Billie learned that the woman who had stopped the potential stampede was human rights activist and anti-violence leader Erica Ford. The right person in the right place at the exact right moment—"for just such a time as this" (Esther 4:14). Like Norea, Erica cried out and was received. And like Norea, she spoke from her deep rootedness in herself, in her own wholeness, and from a divinity that she possessed before she, and this world, came into being.

NOREA'S WAY TO SAVE THE UNITED STATES FROM GUNS

One of the most devastating parts of the COVID-19 pandemic in the United States has been the way Americans bought millions more guns for their private use against one another.

Glenn Thrush of the *New York Times* wrote on May 17, 2022: "Two manufacturers are dominating the handgun market, the report said. Smith & Wesson accounted for 8.2 million guns produced from 2016 to 2020, 17 percent of the overall market, and Sturm, Ruger & Company was close behind, with nearly identical sales and production figures."

The third unsettled period began in 2019 and extended through the 2020 election and pandemic.

Gun production increased across the board during that time. But demand for semi-automatic handguns rose at the fastest rate on record, with pistol production rocketing from around three million to 5.5 million annually, the report found.

The number of imported guns of all types has also been rising sharply, doubling from around two million per year a decade ago to more than four million in 2020, a record.

Many of those were first-time buyers who flooded The Bureau of Alcohol, Tobacco, Firearms and Explosives' (ATF) switchboard and email servers for information about how to buy a gun legally, and which weapons were best for personal protection, one ATF official said.

Under cover, the Ancient Savior Norea has begun to organize a national grassroots action for the peaceful elimination of firearms by private citizens. Norea has appeared from time to time in the world to eliminate violence and establish peace. Known primarily for her success in assertive elimination of rape in imperial settings, Norea also has sometimes disappeared for centuries at a time. Some think that this has to do with her intense devotion to deep peace, and that she needs to live near the ocean or in the woods for a long time to develop a strength that has no aggression in it.

This antigun action in the United States depends on intense collaboration between countrywide community action, local governments, state governments, and federal government in buying back guns from all local gun owners. Many have just laughed at Norea as a real leader that can have enough creativity, patience, and strength to change America's inherent need for materiality and violence.

But it turns out that Norea is one of the only divine saviors who can generate her own divinity for particularly impossible tasks. This means that Norea can generate divinity for humans as well, so that her self-generating divine spirit becomes present in massive groups of people. Just like Mahatma Gandhi's spirit gave this same self-generating spirit of peace to millions and millions of Indians, so Norea, *"Voice of Truth, upright Mind"* (*The Thought of Norea* 27:16–17), can enter its own divinity into millions of Americans in order to transform that nation away from gun-based violence.

Celene Lillie's insight into Norea lets us see how she transforms humans so that they join Norea in:

> how people act in the face of the (evil) rulers . . . they
> refuse to participate in their actions, and they should not

be afraid to ask for assistance . . . (Norea) is not distracted by their . . . violence . . . Norea has freed herself from: "the bondage of the authorities error" (*Reality of the Rulers* 93:6, 7) . . . Norea, by embodying the qualities of those who come from the Father, provided a model for humanity to follow.[2]

---

[2] Celene Lillie, *The Rape of Eve* (Fortress Press, 2017), 268.

Papyrus fragment:
Papyrus 27

THE ODES OF
SOLOMON

Where discovered: Scholar, J. R. Harris, who found the texts, doesn't remember when or where he came across this text.

When discovered: This text was rediscovered in 1909 when scholar J. R. Harris found the papyrus while cleaning out his study.

Length: At forty-one odes and at a third of the size of Psalms, this text is one of the largest collections of early Jesus groups' worship material found intact.

Interesting fact: Wikipedia will tell you there are forty-two odes in this collection, and the odes are numbered through forty-two, but the text skips from Ode 1 to Ode 3. Ode 2 remains missing.

ABOUT *THE ODES OF SOLOMON*

Of the eight different writings from early Jesus peoples introduced in this book, we have been transfixed by this set of songs from the first two centuries. These songs have been beautifully and powerfully read and sung for our twenty-first century. A number of contemporary recordings of these Odes are on the market: "Odes of Solomon: Mystical Songs from the Time of Jesus" by John Davidson; "The Odes Project" by John Andrew Schreiner, Fernando Ortega, Keith and Krystyn Getty; and "Songs of Your Truth" by Natalie Renee Perkins.

The Odes of Solomon are probably a collection of early Jesus peoples worship material dating back to the first and second centuries. Since some early Jesus and other peoples did not call themselves "Christian" in the first and second century, it might be an error to think of them as "Christian." They were discovered in the early 1900s. While some of these Odes were quite clearly songs, others may have been acted out by a group and many parts of these appear to describe Jesus, while others are a dialogue between the speaker/singer/group and Christ. Although it is not clear whether these ancient songs and plays were performed by Jesus or by his followers in the one to five generations after Jesus, they convey ancient stories about Jesus and beautiful poems.

One more note deserves to be made here as the power of these Odes unfold. Why are these called *The Odes of Solomon*?

The simple answer is that this is the wrong title and they have nothing to do with Solomon. It is clear from the Odes themselves that they were written within or right after the life of Jesus. They should be called something like "The Songs in the Key of Jesus." But they are not. Think of Jesus people now and then as you claim these beautiful odes.

The *Odes* are yet another example of how the writing from the very early Jesus people that had been lost for more than 1,500 years sounds as if it was written in the twenty-first century just for us. This writing of forty-one odes is both very familiar and—at the same time—very fresh and different.

First, please read this slowly to see if it feels helpful for our day. Then reflect on it some more for our time.

Then Generosity hastened again. . . .

Sons and daughters of humanity,
Return yourselves and come.
Abandon the ways of that Corruptor,
And come near to me.
He led you into wrong, but I will bring you out from ruin,
And make you wise in the ways of Truth.
Do not be corrupted, nor perish.
Hear me and be saved,
For I have spoken the generosity of the Lord among you . . .
(33:1, 6–10)

This writing begins and ends with one evocative—yet underused—word for today: "generosity." One need only turn on the news or open Twitter to see the disconnect from a generous mindset. In the United States, the gap between rich and poor has been growing exponentially for at least thirty years. Frankly, encountering generosity today is surprising. Perhaps for this ancient audience, generosity was also a much-needed virtue. This ancient song does not just evoke generosity, "Generosity" is a person who addresses "humanity" and urges humanity to turn drastically and directly toward generous behavior.

Generosity is in such short shrift in the twenty-first century, the first level of reflection may best begin by letting the word "generosity" be the focus. Simply speak it meditatively in order to give it space to live. Say it slowly, letting it sink into consciousness. Perhaps imagining how as individuals generosity can grow. Perhaps thinking how groups, communities, and societies can have generosity expand. Then read the Ode from Generosity silently while listening to some of one's favorite music, and allow generosity to become a new favorite song.

Meditating on Ode 36, translated accurately from the Syriac language of the first or second century, opens up new approaches to connection with this surprising genderfluid Mother God dimension of this ancient song.

I rested on the Spirit of the Lord,
And she raised me up to the high place
And she caused me to stand on my feet in the high place of
    the Lord
Before his fullness and splendor,
While I was proclaiming in the preparation of his odes.

She gave birth to me before the face of the Lord.
And while I was the Child of Humanity
I was called the Light, the Child of God,
Because I was glorified among the glorious,
And first among the great ones.
For she made me according to the greatness of the Most High
And he renewed me according to his renewal,
And anointed me from his fullness.
I became one of those who are near to him
And my mouth was opened like a cloud of dew
And my heart gushed forth a fountain of justice.
And my access was through peace,
And I was set up in the Spirit of Instruction.
Halleluiah.

(36)

And this ancient Ode, written first in the first centuries, portrays deep moments of beauty, goodness, unexpected music, and deep breaths of nature:

I was as the earth which is sprouting and lush in her fruits.
And the Lord is like the sun on the face of the earth.
My eyes . . . illuminated, and my face took in the dew.
My breath was made sweet in the sweet fragrance of the
*   Lord . . .*
In which is the store of the lusciousness of the Lord.
I saw trees that were ripe and bearing fruit and their crown
*   grown naturally.*

Their branches were blooming, and their fruits were beaming . . .

The joyful river irrigates . . . and circles around those of the land of eternal life.

And I said, "Lord, they are blessed, the ones who have planted in your earth . . .

And who grow in the sprouting of your trees, and who turn away from darkness toward the light.

(11:12b–19)

These odes hold in their depths an expansiveness that is connected to the various ways different communities understand God, gender, and beauty and can re-enliven even the most tired of meditative practices.

REFLECTIONS FOR TODAY ON *THE ODES OF SOLOMON*

"MY JOURNEY IS BEAUTIFUL"

When Tash's dear friend died unexpectedly, a small group from the theater community gathered in New York City to remember him and celebrate his life. As a gay black man from Indiana who left to follow his dreams of Broadway, Maurice had filled his thirty-nine years with more life than some who live to old age. They all took turns at the mic to speak about him or sing a song. When Tash spoke she said: "I was with Maurice through some really tough times—some of his darkest moments. We would be walking through the valley of the shadow of death . . . and this man . . . would have the audacity . . . to crack a joke! He could find the joy—the God!—in any situation!"

As the course of anger over irreverence
So also is the course of Joy over the Beloved
Which produces of her fruits without obstacle.
My joy is the Lord and my course is toward him,
My journey is beautiful.
For there is a helper for me, the Lord.
He has made his entire self known to me, without grudge, by
  extension.
Indeed his kindness has shrunk his immensity.
                                        · (*The Odes of Solomon* 7:1–3)

Tasha remembered times she'd occasionally get irritated, wanting Maurice to take the moment more seriously. But as she looked back, she was thankful to Maurice for that tremendous lesson of seeing joy, seeing God in those valley-of-the-shadow-of-death situations. Maurice's life affirmed that God is with her. Even in the worst moments, God is there. ALL of God is there with her, the comforting parts, the joy-filled parts. And God is as easily accessible as she wants God to be. Maurice seemed to have a direct connection to divine joy and love that knew no bounds and seemed to almost seep from his pores. And Maurice shared that divine connection generously. He stayed to course with God and as a result, his journey, with all of its ups and downs, had indeed been beautiful.

Days later, Tasha was unable to travel back to their hometown for his funeral. She was devastated to have to watch the livestream instead. But she could almost hear Maurice whispering to her the jokes he would make at his own funeral.

THIRD GRADE

Lucas sat at his desk in the fourth row of Mrs. Medeiras's class, staring at his worksheet. It was a little blurry from the tears standing in his eyes. For the second time this week, Tommy Rogers had picked on him during recess while Mrs. Medeiras wasn't looking. He was very good at not getting caught. When Lucas told her what happened, she sighed and looked over at Tommy who was now playing a game of tag with some other boys. "Perhaps you should find someone else to play with," she said, and added a warning about tattling. Feeling his frustration rise, he looked down at his shoes and simply replied: "Yes, ma'am."

When they lined up to come in from recess, Tommy ended up in line right behind Lucas. Lucas ignored him but then Tommy pinched Lucas hard on the arm to get his attention and repeated the mean thing he'd been saying all throughout recess about Lucas's shirt looking like he belonged in jail. Lucas loved his striped shirt. He liked the way it looked against his brown skin. It was one of his favorites . . . until now. He didn't dare tell Mrs. Medeiras what happened. Instead he slid down into his chair, blinked back his tears, and tried to focus on his times tables.

When he got home from school, he told his babysitter what had happened. She listened intently as she made them a snack. "He sounds like a real jerk," she said when he'd finished. "Yeah," Lucas replied, taking a bite of his PB&J. He wished someone had warned him that third grade would be this tough.

That night, before bed, he and his dad sang the song they'd written together that was based on a poem his mama used to recite while he was still in her belly. He'd got to meet her but she died shortly after he was born so he didn't really remember. But his dad told Lucas all about her and the dreams she had of and for him. His dad would recite this poem every night to Lucas before he went to sleep and along the way, they had created a melody together. Now his dad brought his guitar with him when he went to tuck Lucas in for the night and they sang the poem instead:

> *I rested on the Spirit of the Lord,*
> *And she raised me up to the high place*
> *And she caused me to stand on my feet in the high place of*
> *   the Lord*
> *Before his fullness and splendor,*
> *While I was proclaiming in the preparation of his odes.*
> *She gave birth to me before the face of the Lord.*
> *And while I was the Child of Humanity*
> *I was called the Light, the Child of God,*
> *Because I was glorified among the glorious,*
> *And first among the great ones.*
>
> (The Odes of Solomon 36:1–3)

"Remember," his daddy said, "you are glorious." He didn't really understand all of what that meant, but tonight it gave him comfort to know that regardless of what dumb old Tommy Rogers said, mommy and daddy and God all thought he was great.

The writer of this ancient ode found their solace in the Spirit of the Lord and felt a close special connection in this relationship. This glorification the writer experienced certainly resonated with Lucas's mom who spoke this into Lucas while he was still in utero, with his dad who carried on this new tradition after Lucas's mother had passed, and is making a home in Lucas's heart. His understanding of this ode will shift as he grows and learns but even at this young age, he is finding solace in the Spirit of the Lord during tough times. This ode has space for all who seek this comfort and the reassurance of a special divine connection.

WATER IS SCRIPTURE

For a stream went out, and became a river, great and broad.
Truly it flooded everything, broke it up, and brought it to the
* Temple.*
Neither were the impediments of humanity able to dam it,
Nor the skills of those who usually restrain waters.
For it came over the whole face of the earth.
And filled everything.
All of the thirsty ones upon the earth drank,
And the thirst was diminished and quenched.
The drink was given from the Most High,
Therefore, happy are the ministers of that drink.
(The Odes of Solomon 6:8–13)

Cecelia didn't realize this until later in life, but she is a water person. She loves to be near the water. She needs to be near water. She currently lives between two rivers—the Hudson River and the Harlem River. A twenty-minute walk in either direction will put her at one of their banks. Her summers are spent trying to fit in as many visits to the beaches of the Atlantic Ocean, or any other ocean, as possible.

There is an unspoken cleansing in the water. She uses it as part of a cleansing ritual at the beginning of each summer season, letting the waves crash over her, take her down, topple her over, rinse thoroughly winter's chill from her bones, purify her with their salt. It forces her body to release the tension she's built up over the nearly year since she last waded into the depths. It tears away exhaustion stored in the little crevices of her being and refreshes her.

There is unspoken wisdom in the water. Wisdom of forebears who were forced to cross those waters. Wisdom of ancestors who refused that passage and chose a watery grave as refuge. Wisdom of people who fled terror in hopes of safe harbor in another country. Water holds and keeps secrets left unknown.

There is unspoken healing in water. It cleanses her body, hydrates her, this thing that baptizes babies and adults alike. It washes away dirt or infection; it keeps all healthy and safe. Sitting near it calms her nervous system and relieves her anxiety.

There is unspoken divinity in the water. It holds the whisper of God, if she sits still enough, if she closes her eyes, if she listens long enough. The water is scripture.

CONTEXT IS KEY

Amari was watching a friend's story on Instagram the other day and one popped up of him driving along. He wrote across it something about how relaxing driving with no destination was. He was out for an hour's drive for relaxation.

She had just recently returned home from a trip to Indianapolis where she'd had to drive nearly every single day for the entire six weeks she was there. From the minute she got on the road in her little rental car, she felt like she was in the Indy 500. Cars whizzed by her at thirty miles an hour over the speed limit. She quickly realized she'd need to drive much faster if she didn't want to be squashed. Folks cut across multiple lanes of highway to take their exit and there always seemed to be a number of abandoned cars on the side of the road during any given drive. She noticed a lot of the cars had dents or major damage as they sped by, and sometimes lights that didn't work. Even her rental endured its fair share of nicks during that time.

The entire city seemed like it was under construction and every road seemed to have a pothole to avoid. It was difficult to navigate the city she'd grown up in. She felt tension from her knuckles to her shoulders and down her spine any time she drove during this trip. She said a little prayer of thanks and breathed a sigh of relief every time she arrived at her destination. She longed for her NYC subway where she could read or listen to something in her headphones, or simply stare off and daydream.

It was never restful. It was never relaxing. It was always stressful.

She replied to her friend's story to tell him just that. She playfully wrote: "This is how I know I'm a New Yorker bcos just driving does not sound relaxing to me at all lol." Her friend, who is also a theologian/scholar/preacher, replied in kind, "See how the context be making all the difference lol."

Context is key. It wasn't whether one of them was right or wrong, but rather what each experienced in the act. It was a difference of approach. It reminded her of part of an ode from one of her books from seminary.

> *You have given us your intimacy;*
> *It was not that you were lost from us,*
> *But rather that we were lost from you.*
>
> (*The Odes of Solomon* 4:9)

These verses highlight a different approach. It wasn't that God hadn't revealed God's self to this ancient audience, but rather that they just didn't see God. As she stared absently at her smart device, she mused. Looking back over her life, she knew God was there in every moment. But, can she say that she always recognized or felt the Presence of the Divine in every moment? No. But context is key. It wasn't because God wasn't there. It was that she only needed to look up.

THE WALK

The generations spoke to one another through him,
And those that were silent were able to speak.
From him came love and worth,
And they spoke, one to the other, that which was theirs.
                                        (*The Odes of Solomon* 12:8–9)

The old woman moved about her home more slowly than she used to, her grandson observed, but still with a sort of deftness that gave away her lifetime of martial arts training. Those days were long gone, but she still practiced Tai Chi in the park with her friends on Monday mornings. The two of them met like this every Wednesday afternoon, GrandmaLu and Eric, for a lunchtime walk as long as the weather was agreeable. His high school was just down the street and he'd started skipping out to walk with GrandmaLu right after Grandpa Joe and his dad died during his freshman year last year. He was a straight A student so no one ever seemed to notice how he quietly slipped in and out of the building once a week. In fact, GrandmaLu was the reason he was still such a good student. Their walks helped him process the car accident that had taken the lives of both men. Plus, she was the smartest person he knew and she got such joy from watching him do well in school. These walks were a secret between just the two of them.

She put her tea cup on the kitchen counter, grabbed the waxed-paper-wrapped sandwich, and shuffled over toward the door where he stood. Taking a seat on the bench nearby, she handed him the sandwich, put on her shoes, glanced at his footwear, and said to him what she always said every Wednesday as she tied her own shoes: "Nice kicks!"

He could practically hear the gleam in her eye. GrandmaLu had bought him these tennis shoes and he always made sure to wear them on Wednesdays. He responded with his weekly line: "Oh, these old things?" And pointed his toes this way and that, showing off the shoes. "Thanks," he said, with a chuckle. "Well, what shall we talk about today?"

"I've learned something new today," she said excitedly as she opened the door. "I'll tell you all about it." She often started their walks like this. At the age of eighty-seven, GrandmaLu maintained a strong thirst for knowledge. She reminded Eric of a children's book his little sister used to read called *The Hungry Caterpillar*. An insatiable reader, she had bought a tablet a few years back so she could read "without accumulating more junk," as she put it, and Eric had helped get her set up. Now, she knew more about the inner workings of that tablet than he did and she was midway through a class on coding, "just for fun," she said, though Eric thought she'd probably taken an interest because of him. Eric loved coding and had fun sharing with GrandmaLu new things he'd learned. It was as if they were comparing notes. They often joked about the two of them going into business together.

As they wrapped up their walk, they hugged on the sidewalk in front of her house. "See you next week, Eric," she said as she made her way up the walk to the door. "Okay, Gma! Love you!" Eric said, glancing back over his shoulder to make sure she made it in the house as he jogged back to school to make it just in time to beat the bell.

The father of Black Liberation theology, James Cone, would say: "it's all 'God talk.'" Every conversation, in the words spoken and the silence in between, from the most mundane to the most abstract, is full of the divine and how we understand God. The bonds created by relation and strengthened by a shared tragedy make endearing the Divine Love spoken in conversation that can only belong to them during a sweet, simple, intergenerational afternoon walk. These conversations litter everyday life, filling this world with God's love.

GOD IS THERE

Indigo describes herself as a multihyphenate—working in entertainment and religion. One of her favorite things about her religious work is listening to people share about their experiences with God. She loves to hear where people meet God. It's often done in many different ways. There's a passage from the *Odes of Solomon* that really resonates with her as she thinks about this.

> *Keep my mystery, you who are kept by it.*
> *Keep my faith, you who are kept by it.*
> *Recognize my knowledge, you who, in truth, know me.*
> *Love me with gentleness, those who love.*
> (*The Odes of Solomon* 8:10–11)

For instance, she met God in a song long before she even knew what it was. The transcendence that occurs in music reveals the mystery of the Divine. She also met God in her scholastic endeavors while studying texts and learning translations, examining different theologies and religions. Each new revelation seems like another window opens, allowing more fresh air and a different viewpoint that expands her understanding of God.

A student at the college where she serves as chaplain explained to her how they met God through a kernel of faith the size of a mustard seed. When they weren't sure what was going to happen and what else to do, they trusted in some resources they'd worked on together and God met them there.

And Indigo recently listened to the story from a Black lesbian couple about how they met God while falling in love with each other. Loving another person so deeply expanded their understanding and capacity for love and, in doing so, revealed the Divine.

Each of these examples are so different, each experience unique, yet all lead to a similar outcome. The ode speaks of mystery, faith, knowledge, and love as the connecting points to the Divine. God is there—in the mystery, in the faith, in the knowledge, in the love—in the midst and will meet all at the core and depths of those willing.

"MY HEART GUSHED FORTH"

It was the first time they would hold the clan dance in a public park. She, of course, knew these dances well. By fourteen, she had practiced them since she was three. Her mother had made the turtle shell panels on her leggings first when she was five, and she was so proud of how they looked as they danced. Her father had told her time and again how so much depended on learning and keeping the dances. And by her eighth birthday she had joined her mother in connecting the shells along her legs and learned to shake them in Muscogee rhythm. By the time she was ten she was leading the regular Wednesday evening sessions in the tribal clubhouse on the outskirts of their small city in the panhandle of Florida. Even though there were at least four elders five times her age, they knew that she could lead at least ten of the dances.

Of course, in school there were lots of white kids who made fun of her if she wore her native braids. Especially those boys who would sometimes pull on her braids. But she felt mostly safe since the fourteen-year-old boys from the clan also had beautiful long braids and very strong arm muscles.

But today as she thought about the dance being in the city park, she did wonder whether those white boys would be there too. And as she thought about them and how mean they were to her, she remembered stories of her grandfather as a young boy, when his schoolteacher beat him whenever he spoke Muscogee instead of English. He still taught her their native language

As they drove toward the city park, she remembered how important it would be to focus on an inner peace and on how the turtle shell sound would make her strong. As she and her people gathered in the circle dance, their chanting carried them together.

But then she felt a rock hit her leg. She looked around but could not see anyone. Then more rocks came and she realized that they were coming from the woods at the edge of the field. Immediately she remembered the camera in her cell phone. She still kept herself in the circle dance motion, but she circled wider toward the woods. As the white boys saw her swinging more widely toward them, they kept throwing the rocks and came out of the woods and stood there. She shook her shells harder and swung in an even wider circle.

She could still feel her circling Muscogee people carrying her peacefully. As she reached the nearest angle to the white boys, she suddenly danced more loudly and held her cell phone camera high pointing toward the white kids, taking pictures of them, using the camera's flash to make sure they knew that she was taking their pictures.

They stopped throwing the stones, now fearing that pictures of them would get them in trouble. She now had stopped moving past them, but simply continued her dancing while standing near them and photographing them. She shouted her dance chant loudly and so did all the dancers. Without waiting any more, the white boys turned and ran, while the dancers swung their legs with the turtle shells and kept singing. Now all the dancers were circling and alive with their triumph dance.

And my mouth was open like a cloud of dew, and my heart gushed forth a fountain of justice. And my access was through peace. And I was set up in the Spirit of Instruction. Halleluiah! (The Odes of Solomon 36:6, 7)

This Muscogee teenager clearly had her mouth open like a cloud of dew as she celebrated the beauty of her people's dance. Her heart also gushed forth like a fountain of justice as she stood up to the stone-throning boys. It was through peace itself that she had access to joy and courage. She rose in knowing who she and her people have always been when they dance and sing.

THE WEIGHT OF THE CROWN

Shay held this Howard Thurman quote near and dear to their heart all through undergrad and law school: "A crown is placed over our heads that for the rest of our lives we are trying to grow tall enough to wear." Now as Shay prepared for the bar exam, they recited the quote.

Shay would be the first lawyer in their family, the first Black lawyer in their community. Justice had always been so important to Shay, it didn't surprise anyone when they pursued a law degree. Just on the other side of this exam was an amazing position at a prestigious law firm whose focus was civil rights cases.

Shay sat back in their chair and rubbed their eyes. It was one a.m. The exam was less than a week away. Shay glanced over at the book their artsy brother had given them. He was always trying to get Shay to connect to their more creative self. He told Shay it was a book of ancient songs and poems. Shay would read it sometimes when they needed a break. Shay flipped now to their favorite passage.

> *Truth is an eternal crown,*
> *Happy are those who set it upon their head.*
> *It is a precious, heavy stone,*
> *In fact the wars were because of the crown.*
> *Justice has taken it,*
> *And given it to you.*

> (*The Odes of Solomon* 9:8–10)

Shay closed the book and thought about the quote by Thurman. For a moment, Shay held the image in their mind of the crown of truth just above their head, with Lady Justice holding it steady, waiting for them. The universal importance and sovereignty of truth permeates from our earliest writings all the way through to today. In a week, Shay would be ready to start the lifetime journey of honoring and upholding truth.

TWO JOURNEYS IN PRISON

It felt like he would never get out. This was the second time he'd been in. His bid was only four years, which was eighteen more months than the first one. But still, if he could stay more or less clean, he could still have a chance in the real world. He knew this time he was wrong. Not like the first time when he had been innocent. But there were so many vicious things that the COs did to the cellies that he was afraid he might go 5150.* Better off to be a programmer,** but no reason to ride leg.*** It is true that being a programmer had its risks too. The key was simply to stay as clean as he could, so he'd have a chance for a job when he got out. He really did feel bad about stealing from the grocery store. Should he make a full confession? He'd already been beaten twice for being too good.

A YOUNG MAN IN A SECOND-CENTURY ROMAN PRISON

I opened the doors which were shut.
I destroyed the bars of iron,
Since my own irons . . . melted away before me.
Nothing appeared closed to me anymore,

---

* 5150 refers to the California law code for the temporary, involuntary psychiatric commitment of individuals who present a danger to themselves or others due to signs of mental illness. It has been more generally applied to people who are considered threateningly unstable or "crazy."

** An inmate who spends most of his time attending classes and improving himself: the nerds of prison.

*** To suck up to prison staff to get favors.

Because I was the opening of everything.
I turned toward all my captors, in order to dissolve them,
So that I would not leave anyone bound or binding. . . .
(*The Odes of Solomon* 17:9–12)

This comparison between being jailed in a twenty-first-century US prison and one under the thumb of the Roman Empire in the second century shows how similar their plights were. Each is in major danger. But somehow the person imprisoned by Rome has been able to escape, which has opened everything up. The American prisoner is still under the threat of both fellow prisoners and prison guards.

Jesus's imprisonment by Rome ended with his torture to death by crucifixion. The Jesus people produced this song about the prisoner who broke free of prison and all of a sudden everything opened up, although Jesus himself did not get to go free.

GETTING READY

Tobi's anxiety was mounting. It had been for a long time, but finally actually making the doctor's appointment to talk about transitioning made the whole thing more real. They knew they were just at the beginning of a long and important journey, but fear of rejection from friends and family was mounting. Tobi had kept their desire to transition from their family and everyone in their community, quietly saving money while settling for painting their nails fun colors and piling their long dark locks into a messy bun on top of their head.

Every Sunday, Tobi stood up on a platform stage at the front of a large auditorium full of people to lead the congregation in Praise and Worship at the beginning service. Tobi served on a team of people at this church whom Tobi was afraid would say: "We love you and respect your decision," but would come back later, as Tobi was transitioning, and say: "We don't think it is a good idea to have you serve in a leadership position at the church anymore." Tobi shuddered at this thought. They deeply loved their ministry work as an expression of their love for the Lord. Also Tobi was afraid of losing their job when they needed their insurance more than ever for this journey.

Tobi was surrounded by people who referred to being gay as a "lifestyle choice." If that's what they thought about sexuality, Tobi couldn't imagine this community could accept a gender transition. Tobi had watched their father try to convince their uncle, using "clobber texts" from the Bible, that homosexuality was a sin and that he must turn away from this life to avoid eternal damnation. Tobi's father had begged and pleaded with Tobi's uncle. After that, Tobi's uncle no longer spoke to the family. But Tobi was still connected with him on Facebook. Their uncle seemed happy and he'd found a welcoming and affirming church community.

Still Tobi worried. Would they lose their church community, and maybe even their family?

Tobi absent-mindedly noodled on the guitar while thinking it through. They'd recently come across an ode in a collection of ancient Christian worship material that they couldn't get out of their mind. They shifted a couple of the words and rearranged some others and suddenly, Tobi had a song.

Look! the Lord God is our mirror,
Open your eyes and see God in them.
Learn the manner of your faces,
And announce to God's spirit: praises.
Wipe the dirt from your faces.
Love the Lord's holiness and put it on.
Then you will not, at any time, be blemished in front of God.
Halleluiah.

(*The Odes of Solomon* 13)

Tobi didn't know what would happen on this journey but no matter what happened, they knew that God saw them. Tobi knew they were not blemished in front of God. And Tobi prayed that people would see God in Tobi's eyes, in Tobi's whole being as it changed in the coming years. This body didn't fit; it had never felt like Tobi. They had come to terms with that. They had found community online to help think through what that meant and what to do.

Tobi didn't know what would happen with their church community—if they'd resist changing pronouns, insist on deadnaming them, pressure Tobi into some very uncomfortable conversations, hold Tobi at arm's length. But Tobi knew this was a journey they needed to take. Tobi wasn't ready but was working on getting there. Tobi saw this transition as becoming more themself, as the ode said, "wiping the dirt from their face" so that the mirror of God was more visible.

As Tobi got ready for rehearsal with the band, they threw on a slim black tunic that went down to their knees over ripped faded jeans. Tobi added a red plaid flannel over top and slung the guitar strap across their shoulder. Tobi decided that today, they would teach the Praise and Worship team this song.

The image of God is always visible in each person. If toxic ideologies—in this instance, transphobia—were wiped away, the image of God would be easier to see. In this story, Tobi has opened their eyes and found the image of God within them, regardless of the body they were born into. Many around this country and world go bravely into communities that may not accept them or have already rejected them, knowing that they are not blemished in front of God.

BURNOUT'S ANECDOTE

Kim worked hard for the movement. She marched, she shouted, she circulated petitions, she met with city officials, she wrote letters, she passed on templates, she . . .

She worked hard for her family. She prepped meals, arranged pickups and playdates, took her father to his doctor's appointments, did laundry, kept the house relatively clean in the event of what her and her husband jokingly called a "judgmental driveby" from his mother, she . . .

She worked hard for her church. Was asked to be on six committees this year because she's "such a good laborer for the Lord," helped organize and execute Women's Day, Children's Day, the Usher Board's Sunday, and the three-day revival. She . . .

Kim didn't go to bed at night; she simply passed out. She didn't eat her food; she inhaled it. She didn't talk to people; she quizzed them, trying to get to the useful part of the conversation as quickly as possible.

She was burned out. All the way out.

A friend, a senior minister of a large church, invited her to Atlanta for an extended weekend. Her friend reminded her: "Kim, you must play as hard as you work." They went to a day spa to relax. It took her four hours, several hot tub sessions, a slow lunch, and a massage before she felt herself melt into relaxation. She lay down on the cushioned floor and fell asleep. It was the best rest she'd had in a while. She slept so long that her friend thought to wake her but then let her sleep until she awoke naturally.

It came to Kim in a dream:

Comfort has been revealed for your salvation.
Trust and live and be saved.
Halleluiah.

(The Odes of Solomon 34:6)

When Kim awoke, she realized she'd fallen asleep staring at these words inscribed on the wall she was facing. In her newly refreshed state, she remembered that her sacrifice is not salvific. She was of little good to anyone if she was not good to herself. She decided right then and there on that cushioned floor that comfort, peace, and rest would be her salvation.

A SPIRITUAL PRACTICE

Charlotte was learning things so mind blowing that it completely shifted the way she thought about everything. Since starting college, she'd met so many different people from all different kinds of backgrounds. She'd been immersed in so many new ideas. She was learning so much without even trying. It was like taking a morning walk through a tall grass field back home. When the grass was covered with dew, you couldn't help but get wet. She'd recently jumped into educating herself on social justice issues, particularly around race, and she couldn't believe all of the ways race impacted society! Her father had always told her racism wasn't real. "Hell, some of them have it better than we do!"

But now, she felt like when Saul became Paul in the Bible. It was like scales had fallen from her eyes and her heart broke for people who had been treated differently by banks, by the government, by doctors, by their neighbors, by police, simply because of the color of their skin. She felt ashamed about the part she'd played in this—the way she'd looked down on people of color in her neighborhood, the way she'd laughed at racist jokes, the way she'd dismissed the slightest question in her heart over the years when things didn't seem to add up on the news. The cracking open of her heart was painful but it also seemed to allow for a new energy for justice. She wanted to do like that cool quote she saw on that upperclassmen's sweatshirt: "Be the change you wish to see in the world."

She was so moved by a bit of poetry she found in a book in the student lounge:

And my mouth was open like a cloud of dew
And my heart gushed forth a fountain of justice.
And my access was through peace,
And I was set up in the Spirit of Instruction.
Halleluiah.

(*The Odes of Solomon* 36:6–7)

She met with the school chaplain who told her to consider making anti-racism part of her spiritual practice. She knew she had a long journey ahead of her. She winced a little at the thought of going home at the end of the semester and what her father and brother would say about her new views on society. She could already hear her dad call her a snowflake and say that he knew that college would turn her into a social justice warrior. She could already hear her brother joke about her being the "PC Police" and ask for her badge. She could hear it because she had said these things herself about others in the past. But she decided that none of that would stop her. She was full of energy and wanted to make sure she was deeply rooted in knowledge.

The odist of this ancient text wasn't hesitant in the least to access justice through peace. Even though this writer mentions it last, a foundation of learning is key to being able to do all the rest. Though at the beginning of a long and sometimes rough road, Charlotte seems poised to do this as well.

STRONGER THAN YESTERDAY

Imagine late night in a dark, haze-filled jazz club. Musicians gather once a week to hone their skills, to play with different combos and different people, to experiment. A woman walks up to the stage area, which is really just a space in front where the tables have been pushed aside. She whispers to the musicians who nod, intrigued. She then steps up to an empty mic where the soloing horn player normally stands. Usually there aren't singers, but he scoots aside to allow her space. The band plays a walk-down introduction that's a little crunchier, a little dirtier than what they've been playing. It sounds more like blues. The woman opens her mouth, releasing a wail—somewhere between a riff and a plea. She pauses and the low din of murmuring is gone. Even the clinking of glasses from the bartenders has halted; the consistently dripping faucet seems to hold its drop. The wail escapes her painted red lips again, seeming to come from the depths of her soul: *"Lord, I profess you . . ."* (*The Odes of Solomon* 5:1a)

The band remembers they are there and kicks back in, filling four beats, then silence again.

"Because, because, because," the singer starts and, seemingly frustrated with not being able to land on words big enough to describe why, she lands on *"because I love you."*

"Most High," she begs, *"do not abandon me."* (*The Odes of Solomon* 5:1b–2a) The band picks up for another four hits.

"Because you are my hope." (*The Odes of Solomon* 5:2b) The band settles in with her into dirty blues.

I freely receive your kindness
May I be kept alive by it
My tormentors will come; do not let them see me
Let a cloud of darkness fall over their eyes
And a vapor of dark mist eclipse them.

(The Odes of Solomon 5:3–5)

She lifts her hand and drags it across the air, as if she is conjuring up this dark mist. It is only then that you notice the shiner surrounding her left eye that makeup did little to cover. She sings,

And let there be no light, no light
For them by which they might see
So that they will not seize me.
Let their minds become swollen, swollen!
And let whatever they have devised return upon their heads.
Truly they have devised a judgment
But it was not for them to do
They prepared themselves wickedly
And they were found empty (The Odes of Solomon 5:6–9)

As she holds that last note, her arms rise from her sides, hands splayed and head leaning back toward the ceiling as if she's singing to the sky. It is only then that you notice the track marks in her right arm.

Indeed, my hope is upon the Lord.
I will not fear
Because the Lord is my redemption.

I will not fear.
He is a crown upon my head
I will not be moved
If everything else should be shaken
I will stand
If what's visible should perish
I will not die
Because the Lord is with me
And I am with him. (The Odes of Solomon 5:10–15)
And I am with him.
And I am with him.

The band stops playing.

She sings alone, almost with the same pleading sound from earlier—loud, weary, but determined: "I will not die."

There is a stunned silence before the room erupts in applause. She trembles a bit as she leaves the playing area. Her shoe catches the frayed carpet and she stumbles a little. When she looks down to catch herself, it causes her hair to fall over her face. It is only then that you notice the bruising around her neck.

Despite the obviously difficult life this woman is living, she is fighting still to live it. Like the writer of the ancient ode sings, she refuses to give up. This story doesn't give any clues as to how the woman came to know and sing this ancient ode but there seems to be, on both ends, plenty of dangers, toils, and snares along their paths. Yet, both of them, through a song sung thousands of years apart, fight hard to claim their tomorrows.

DEALING WITH TORMENTORS

The Odes of Solomon takes on a huge problem for some of the earliest Jesus people of the first and second centuries. The problem in this ancient book's own words is that there are tormentors in that ancient world that came at many ordinary people with designs to make life hard for them and in some cases to kill them. Many of these tormentors were official police people and soldiers whose job it was to torment many people who were not doing anything that deserved this violent and constant tormenting.

This is true today in the United States too. There are thousands of such tormentors who give themselves over to make life hard, frightening, and dangerous for Black people, brown people, Native people, queer people, and other marginalized people. Many of you are being tormented in this way, many of you may not be tormented but are very distressed by how many professional government tormentors successfully make deep trouble for so many others, and many have not had to deal with these tormentors in this country.

Ode 5 holds up seven different ways to resist the tormentors:

- Cry and pray to God not to be abandoned as the tormentors come at so many ordinary people. (*The Odes of Solomon* 5:2)
- Be thankful to God for God's kindness in resisting the tormentors. (*The Odes of Solomon* 5:3)
- Be ready for the tormentors. (*The Odes of Solomon* 5:4)
- Wish and hope that the tormentors do not see the people

they want to torment, that a cloud of darkness fall over the tormentors' eyes, and that a dark mist eclipse the tormentors. (*The Odes of Solomon* 5:5–7)

- But these people hope in God. (*The Odes of Solomon* 5:10)
- Do not be afraid of the tormentors because God is redeeming the people who are tormenting them, because God is a crown on the people in danger, and those people will try not to be shaken or moved. (*The Odes of Solomon* 5:11, 12)
- Be with God, and let God come to those who are tormenting. (*The Odes of Solomon* 5:15)

There is no one solution for those who are physically, mentally, spiritually, and psychologically tormented, whether that happened in the first two centuries of the Jesus peoples or in the twenty-first century. The horror of terror is so deep and difficult that to survive it, people must have a number of skills, strengths, and connections to others and to nature. For those tortured now and earlier, those who are close to people who are tortured, and those who support those tortured far away, the suggestions above in Ode 5 have merits.

DANCING WITH THE LORD

"What do I open my heart to? How do I let God in? Even as I constantly open myself up to new experiences of God, I also think, 'ehhhh, but is that cool enough, or meaningful enough, or serious enough, or perfect enough?'"

Rev. Samuel had become accustomed to preaching on Zoom, situated at a desk she'd set up in front of her living room window to optimize the light. She looked at her screen. Full of the congregation she adored. Seeing their exhaustion of countless hours spent on Zoom—in meetings, in worship, at lectures, in gatherings—staring at their screen.

"Yeah, you heard that right—or *perfect* enough.

That's a mighty high bar.

Doesn't leave much space for dancing joy. It does, however, leave space for dental bills because I grind my teeth to dust from the pressure of perfection. Take a look at this scripture passage."

She switched to screen share and these words came across the screen:

Open; open your hearts to the dancing joy of the Lord
And let your love abound from heart to lips:
In order to bring forth fruit of the Lord, a holy life
And speak with attention in his light.
Stand and be restored,
All of you who were once flattened.
Speak, you who were silent,
Because your mouth has been opened.
From now on be lifted up, you who were destroyed

Since your justice has been raised.
For the Right Hand of the Lord is with you all,
And she will be a helper for you.
Peace was prepared for you,
Before what may be your war. (*The Odes of Solomon* 8:1–7)

"This odist," she said, "calls us to open our hearts to the dancing joy of the Lord. The moves that might not land right on the beat, bump up against the enclosure, cracking your heart open just a little bit more. The wacky waving arms tickling the edges, coaxing them out a little more. It seems that for them, only then can love held in the heart make it to the lips. It seems as if making space for this kind of messy uninhibited dancing joy is *essential* for a holy life. The odist speaks of restoration and of peace even before times of trouble or hard work."

She ended the screen share and continued: "Right in the midst of these things, the peace is there because we are rooted in joy. It reminds me of a song—'This joy that I have, the world didn't give it to me. The world didn't give it and the world can't take it away.' What would we learn if we took even a little break from the preconceived notions of what it's all supposed to look like and just gave into dancing joy? Now, if you'll excuse me, I'm gonna test this out for myself, starting with a dance party right here in my living room. I hope you'll join me."

She shared her sound to Zoom and pressed play on a recording she'd found of this ode—an uptempo with horns, a full chorus, and clapping. She got out of her chair and began to dance. And to her hopeful delight, she watched as her congregants got out of their seats and danced to the joy of the Lord with her.

OLYMPIC TRIALS AND TRIBULATIONS

Ani sat there, pushing aside embarrassment. This was not her fault and she'd done nothing wrong, she reminded herself. She'd qualified for the Olympic Games fair and square. Her qualifying times were FAST and she was proud of that. She'd worked her butt off to get there and it was not going to end here in this random doctor's office clear on the other side of the world.

She glanced anxiously toward the door. This was all because of those transphobic runners from that other country. She knew it the minute they laid eyes on each other. The whispers, the pointing, the all too familiar feeling of being "othered." Her eyes finally rested on an old copy of an *Olympic Review* magazine. Surprisingly, it was written in her language! She flipped through the pages and landed on a picture of a person in full gear holding a snowboard in one hand. She couldn't tell their gender but it seemed to be a profile piece on them. In the bottom left-hand corner of the picture was a quote:

I was not rejected, nor was I believed to be.
And I did not perish, though they wished it upon me.
(*The Odes of Solomon* 42:10)

She closed the magazine, put it back on the table next to her, and let out a deep breath. She had done all she was supposed to do and she had not been rejected. Her father had always wanted to get this far as a runner, but a knee injury had abruptly ended his career. When she'd come to him in tears about how being trans might affect a career in racing, he'd told her to push through and run on to see what the end would be. He believed in her and had helped her battle every transphobic rule and official she'd come across so far.

But he wasn't here now; she was alone on the other side of the globe. And she knew that look in those other runners' eyes. But, like that quote said, she would not perish, though they probably wished she would. She deserved to be here. She had every right to be here. She didn't know what the IOC would do after this "randomized drug test," but she knew this wasn't about performance-enhancing drugs and besides, she was clean anyway. And she knew she was where she belonged. She knew that she, just like everyone else there, had earned the right to run.

SOOTHED BY THE SPRING

Willy has not had a day off from his city job picking up trash for three weeks. Zaliya needs her job at the restaurant, but half of her colleagues there have quit, and she is on her last leg. In many hospitals, the work of nurses and nurse aides simply never ends. Yet, they are so proud of their work and they know that they are each saving actual lives at least once a week. Similarly, so many doctors have not had a day off in three weeks. Teachers have so many missing colleagues that they are afraid for the children's health in the classroom with not enough workers.

Pressure from all sides is so great on these people that many are not eating well, not exercising well, are short-tempered, and are depressed. Willy feels lonely even in the middle of crowds. Zaliya has been hanging in there, but she worries about other times in her life when she was addicted alternately to too much food and drink. Almost certainly tens of thousands of people in these kinds of times have simply dried up inside.

The ancient Ode 30 holds up a way of coping and renewing in times of stress, pain, and aloneness:

Draw up for yourselves water from the living fountain of the Lord, because it has been opened for you. Come all of you thirsty ones, and take a drink and be soothed by the spring . . . because it is beautiful and clean and restores the self. Indeed its waters are much sweeter than honey, and the honeycomb of bees does not compare with it. . . . They are blessed, those who have drunk from it, and who have been soothed by it. (The Odes of Solomon 30)

But one may reasonably ask, who at the edge of falling apart because of pressure at work and home has a soothing spring of water in nearby nature? Or even say, it is clear that many of us literally cannot afford to take off from work and family chores in order to find such living water. On the other hand, who knows? Perhaps taking time off to find the soothing stream could bring perspective and renewal that may be a key to us at our wits' end.

HARRIET TUBMAN SINGS THE ODES

Harriett Tubman, born into slavery in Maryland, was one of the most powerful and spirit-filled leaders of Black people's march toward freedom throughout most of the nineteenth century and into the twentieth century. She escaped from slavery at twenty-five years of age to Philadelphia, later moved to New York state, and then to Canada. She was a key inspiration in the Underground Railroad, making thirteen trips back into slavery territories to free many enslaved people. She worked for the Union army during the Civil War and was the first woman to lead an armed unit that freed more than 700 enslaved people. For decades after the war, she was a national and international suffragist, speaking and leading women toward the right to vote. For her nearly 100 years, she had many important dreams and understood herself to be "consulting" directly with God.

Strikingly, Ode 8 of *The Odes of Solomon,* written probably in the late first- and early second-century CE, sound now as if Harriett Tubman spoke as long ago as the first or second century:

Stand and be restored,
All of you who were once flattened.
Speak, you who were silent,
Because your mouth has been opened.
From now on be lifted up, you who were destroyed
Since your justice has been raised.

(*The Odes of Solomon* 8:3–5)

May she continue to speak and call people from the first century to the twenty-first century.

Papyrus fragment:
Papyrus Oxyrhynchus 3929

THE PRAYER OF
THANKSGIVING

Where discovered: *The Prayer of Thanksgiving* was found in the jar now referred to as the Nag Hammadi Library.

When discovered: Like *The Gospel of Thomas, The Thunder: Perfect Mind, The Gospel of Truth,* and some forty-eight other Jesus peoples' writings; *The Prayer of Thanksgiving* was discovered in 1945.

Length: Five papyrus pieces of paper in forty-seven lines

Interesting fact: Numerous versions of this prayer were probably practiced by a wide range of people as a part of festive meals. However, this particular written version of this prayer specifically indicates that those who prayed it together did it as a part of devotion to the God of Israel, making it quite likely that Jesus people prayed it.

ABOUT *THE PRAYER*
OF THANKSGIVING

This writing on *The Prayer of Thanksgiving* helps turn a major corner in understanding the way prayer was practiced in the first two centuries of the early Jesus people. Instead of people praying in churches, in their bedroom, or in a small quiet place as they do now and have done for the past three centuries in the United States, at the time of Jesus and for the two hundred years thereafter, probably the main place that people prayed was in festive meals of ten to (at most) twenty-five people.

Even more surprising for these early Jesus times, these festive meals took place with everyone lying down. Sometimes their couches had enough space for two people to lie together. It is true that there were a number of prayers in this setting, but it was generally not a quiet setting; rather, it was a joyful—even boisterous—setting with lots of eating, drinking, conversation, and singing.

What is particularly enlightening about this particular vital combination of prayer and a meal of two to three hours is that the writing itself contains an entire group prayer and then makes clear what the setting was:

When they said these things in prayer, they welcomed one another, and they went to eat their holy food, which had no blood in it. (1:13)

In addition to its lush surrounding of a meal, the prayer was mostly about a creative and intense relationship to God. And it shows how the early Jesus people regularly looked for new language with which to pray. Their relational prayer had them all speaking and praying together about *"the kindness of the Father, and love and desire . . ."* (1:2).

Here are key parts of the prayer where these relational dimensions of God were particularly powerful in the second and third centuries and that have fascinated twenty-first-century readers of this *Prayer of Thanksgiving*:

- *"We rejoice that in the body you have made us divine . . ."* (1:5)
This prayer identified how God's body made humans divine. It does not say for sure that the praying itself made people divine, but that could have been part of what made these humans divine. One dimension of this relational and bodily prayer was that it was done entirely as a group. Unlike modern prayer, which is often individual, these prayers of Jesus people were communal.

- *"O womb of all that grows, we have known you."* (1:8)
In this ancient portrait of God, God explicitly has a womb. More specifically, God's womb makes everything in the universe grow. It is difficult not to connect this ancient prayer of the early Jesus people to the twenty-first-century vision of the universe itself as always growing.

- *"O womb pregnant with the Father, we have known you. O never-ending endurance of the Father who gives birth, so we worship your goodness."* (1:9, 10)

It is deep that the very old writing in 1:8 about a womb-like (female) God is immediately followed with more about God's womb but as God "*the Father who gives birth*." This reminds us that earlier in this book, *The Gospel of Truth* portrays divinity as "*the Father, the Mother, Jesus of boundless sweetness*" (*The Gospel of Truth* 10:6c). And, the Gospel of Luke 7:34–35 calls Jesus "*a friend of tax collectors and sinners . . . and Wisdom, justified by all her children*." In other words, a number of ancient writings of Jesus people —*The Prayer of Thanksgiving*, *The Gospel of Truth*, and the Gospel of Luke—all talk about God and Jesus in terms of female and male at the same time.

REFLECTIONS FOR TODAY ON
THE PRAYER OF THANKSGIVING

WORDS WITH HOPE

Lynn attended two plays recently that were written as letters. It made her think a lot about what feels like a lost form—letter writing. She couldn't remember the last time she put *actual* pen to *actual* paper to write to someone and then *actually* put it in an envelope, addressed it to someone, stamped it, and dropped it in the mail. Oh wait! Yes, she did!

This past winter her castmates from the tour of *Hairspray* she did a number of years ago reconnected on Facebook. They created a direct message group and decided to send each other holiday cards. She had every intention of sending out holiday cards, but she was also in the middle of planning her ordination that was scheduled for December 20. "No worries," she thought to herself. "There's still time after."

Her ordination took place on Zoom in the middle of the COVID-19 pandemic. Her father had contracted the virus and had it pretty bad. The family wore masks in the house and he was quarantined in one part of the house. As her ordination date approached, his doctor cleared him to "attend," which really meant just leaving that portion of the house. According to his doctor, he was no longer contagious. She sat between him and her stepmother during her ordination. On Christmas Day, she woke up sick. She got tested as soon as she was able and, sure enough, she had COVID-19. She dropped everything and focused on her health, quarantining in another part of the house. The holiday cards she was supposed to send were forgotten until she was safely on the other side of quarantine and back home in New York City. It wasn't until she picked up her accumulated mail and saw all of the cards she'd received that she remembered. She decided that since the holidays were long gone, she'd rethink her contribution. She settled on individual letters.

This letter writing gave her an opportunity to speak directly to each person, to celebrate their lives and accomplishments, and to express her gratitude for each friendship. Besides being only a little nervous about her handwriting, writing these letters brought her such unexpected joy! She was able to pray over each individual, filling every page with good energy that she hoped filled them with joy too.

In more ancient times, the aural tradition was how texts were passed along. However, these texts were written as a way to not forget what was important to a community. As a result, we have a collection of letters, prayers, musings, and all sorts of things that tell the story of a people and help to shape contemporary lives of faith. Finding just a portion of anything one has written over their lives would simply not be enough to lay out the full picture. All that has been found of our ancient Christian texts is, likewise, unable to do so. This is important to remember as new materials are encountered.

And if there is a sweet and simple teaching,
it gifts us mind, word, and knowledge:

mind, that we may understand you;
word, that we may interpret you;
knowledge, that we may know you.

(*The Prayer of Thanksgiving* 1:3)

This particular prayer was a letter that filled the page with thanksgiving and hope. May it be received with openness to the insights these extracanonical texts hold for how Christianity, spirituality, the human condition, and individuals can be understood.

YOU HAVE MADE US DIVINE

There are many documents from the Christian New Testament and other writings in which God invites people to think of themselves as divine, just like God and Jesus are. But many people today are surprised to hear that God invites them to think of themselves as a part of God, as divine.

This hesitancy today to take seriously that they are divine probably has to do with later Christian dogma that all humans are sinful to such a degree that God condemns humanity. For instance, even when people today read in the New Testament book of Galatians that "You are all sons of God" (3:26), some today reject humans as divine. Even if human divinity is found often in the New Testament, today's condemnation of humans as inherently evil and full of sin really has made it difficult for people to think well of themselves at all, much less as divine.

Since this *Prayer of Thanksgiving* from the first or second century has some new and intense ways of talking about humans as divine, now would be a good time to consider it. Here are sections of this prayer that speak of how God and humans are connected divinely to one another:

> We give thanks to you God. Every life and heart stretches toward you, O name untroubled . . . To everyone and everything comes the kindness of the Father, and love and desire . . . We rejoice and are enlightened by your knowledge. . . . We rejoice that you have taught us about yourself. We rejoice that in the body you have made us divine through your knowledge. The thanksgiving of the human reaches you is this alone: that

we know you. We have known you. O light of mind, O light of life, we have known you . . . O womb of all that grows, we have known you. O womb pregnant with the nature of the Father, we have known you.

(*The Prayer of Thanksgiving* 1b–9)

The question now is how people can again take in their divinity. Teenangers in the middle of growing up are often thrown into anxiety and unsureness about who they are. Divorcees tumble away from the deep divine life they have lived as others condemn them for the larger brokenness of some marriage life. Poverty slashes at people's strong aliveness inherent in their beauty, humor, and connectedness to each other and nature. Here's to the redemptive ways that life itself and these ancient writings inside and beyond the Bible make so many different humans divine again.

Papyrus fragment:
The Life of Shenoute

ACKNOWLEDGMENTS

TO THOSE, WITH LOVE

And the Most High has given it to the generations:

The expounders of his beauty,
The speakers of his glory,
The confessors of his thought,
And the sanctifiers of his deeds.
The generations spoke to one another through him,
And those that were silent were able to speak.

(The Odes of Solomon 12:4, 8)

Thank you.

To those who see God's beauty all around us and share what you see in such great detail. Who document, record, paint it all to make it plain, to make it visible for all the world to see.

To those who can't help but tell of God's goodness. Who invite us to sing with you how great is our God. Who write stories to explain the sheer magnificence of the Divine.

To those who make a habit, even a job, of explaining ancient texts and ancient civilizations, and how they understood the Divine and how they talked about God in order to expand our knowledge and help us be more discerning.

To those who look at our world and see miracles in the ordinary. Who remind us of the holiness of building a just society. Who see God's work in the work of the people.

How we need your special and very specific gifts as we deepen our own relationships with God. How important you are to shaping a fuller picture of the Divine. Your intergenerational wisdom invites all into the conversation. It expands the boundaries of what our eyes can see to include a little more of God's kin-dom here on earth as it is in heaven.

We have been working together on a wide variety of projects for just short of a decade. Each of us have been hard at work for longer than we care to admit on a wide variety of national projects, with Natalie leading all kinds of theater and musical projects that span everything from acting, composition, creative direction, education, and church. Although Natalie has been on the stage much more than Hal, he has been a professor and pastor on four continents for a long time. Both of us—often together on projects as well as far apart—are fanatics for collaboration and creative working with groups small and large. It's hard to remember how many projects we have done together. And each of us has forced each other and many others to work in the other's primary fields. We are indebted to each other for various learnings along the way.

So it is also intensely the case that each of us has stunning amounts of other collaborators, to whom each of us respectively owes boatloads of credit. Together, a thank you to Adrienne Ingrum and the team at Broadleaf Books for all their work in bringing this book to life.

Hal acknowledges that he is in deep debt to the mountain territories in which he has lived for so long. Specifically he also is healthier and more full of life thanks to Mikayla, Aiden, and Kien.

Natalie would like to specifically thank her families—given and chosen—for their constant and continued love and support.

Prayer in Coptic

ABOUT THE AUTHORS

NATALIE R. PERKINS is a multihyphenate. As a reverend in the United Church of Christ, she is the Minister for Worship and Online Community at Middle Collegiate Church in New York City and serves as a Spiritual Life Advisor at New York University. She received her Master of Divinity from Union Theological Seminary, where she met Hal. She is a cofounder (along with Hal) of Tanho Center, an organization dedicated to incorporating extracanonical texts into contemporary spiritual practices. She has been a contributing writer for *Daily Guideposts* and for *Emancipation Proclamation: Forever Free* as well as a host of other guest devotional contributions in various online collections.

As a creator, Natalie wrote and recorded *Songs of Your Truth*—an EP available on all major music platforms that takes six pieces from *Odes of Solomon* and sets them to contemporary musical genres. As a performer, she has been seen in the national tours of *Hairspray* and *Rent*, has performed around the world on major cruise lines and with the USO Show Troupe, and continues to sing in regional theaters and with symphonies all over the country. Natalie frequently ties both her work in religion and her work in the arts together.

REV. DR. HAL TAUSSIG is a retired professor of New Testament at Union Theological Seminary in New York and a United Methodist pastor. Two of the most recent of his fifteen published books are *After Jesus Before Christianity* and *Re-Reading the Gospel of Mark Amidst Loss and Trauma*. His mediography includes the *New York Times*, *Time*, the *Daily Show*, *People*, *Newsweek*, National Public Radio, the *Los Angeles Times*, the *Philadelphia Inquirer*, the *Brian Lehrer Show* on WNYC, the *Bob Edwards Show* on Sirius Radio, the History Channel, and the *Washington Post*. His world travels as a teacher include Australia, France, Germany, Korea, New Zealand, and Switzerland.

PAPYRUS FRAGMENT CREDITS

Front Matter image
File:Syriac papyri.jpg - Wikimedia Commons
https://upload.wikimedia.org/wikipedia/commons/8/8d/
Syriac_papyri.jpg

Art # 1
Category:Papyrus 15 - Wikimedia Commons
Commons.Wikipedia.org/wiki/Category:Papyrus_15
[15], P^{15}, Papyrus 15 (Gregory-Aland numbering)
Papyrus Oxyrhynchus 1008 (or P. Oxy. 1008, P. Oxy. VII
1008, P. Oxy. 7 1008)

Art #2
Commons.Wikipedia.org/wiki/Category:Papyrus_89
Papyrus Oxyrhynchus 89 (or P. Oxy. 89, P. Oxy. I 89, P. Oxy.
1 89)
Egyptian Museum, Cairo, Cat. Gen. 10008

Art #_3
https://upload.wikimedia.org/wikipedia/commons/9/97/
Padua/Aramaic_1_%28also_known_as_the_Migdol_
papyrus%29.png
Padua Aramaic papyrus 1 (also known as the Migdol papyrus)
- Category:Aramaic papyri - Wikimedia Commons

Art #_4
Category:Apocryphon of John - Wikimedia Commons
https://commons.wikimedia.org/wiki/Category:Apocry-
phon_of_John#/media/File:Apocryphon_of_John.jpg

Art #_5
Category:Gospel of Philip - Wikimedia Commons
https://commons.wikimedia.org/wiki/Category:Gospel_of_
Philip#/media/File:Evangelio_de_Felipe_·_Codex_II,_3_·_
Biblioteca_Copta_de_Nag_Hammadi.png

Art #_6
Category:Gospel of Truth - Wikimedia Commons
https://commons.wikimedia.org/wiki/Category:Gospel_of_
Truth#/media/File
Papiro 17 del Codex I o Code Jung, conteniendo una parte
del Evangelio de la Verdad (NHC I,3) ·- Category:Gospel of
Truth - Wikimedia Commons

Art #_7
Category:Faiyum papyri - Wikimedia Commons
https://commons.wikimedia.org/wiki/Category:Faiyum_
papyri#/media/File: Papyrus_in_Greek_regarding_tax_issues_
(3rd_ca._BC.)_(3210586934).jpg

Art #_8
https://commons.wikimedia.org/wiki/Category:Papyrus 27
- Wikimedia Commons
https://commons.wikimedia.org/wiki/Category:Papy-
rus_27#/media/File:Papyrus_27.png

Art # 9
Category:Papyrus Oxyrhynchus 3929 - Wikimedia Commons
https://commons.wikimedia.org/wiki/Category:Papyrus_
Oxyrhynchus_3929#/media/File:Libellus_scroll.jpg

Art #_10
The Life of Shenoute, Sahidic Coptic script, papyrus, 6th-7th
century CE. From Egypt. British Museum - Category:Coptic
language - Wikimedia Commons
https://commons.wikimedia.org/wiki/Category:Coptic_
language#/media/File:The_Life_of_Shenoute,_Sahidic_
Coptic_script,_papyrus,_6th-7th_century_CE._From_
Egypt._British_Museum.jpg

Art #_11
Padre Nostro copto - Category:Coptic inscriptions - Wikimedia Commons
https://commons.wikimedia.org/wiki/Category:Coptic_
inscriptions#/media/File:Padre_Nostro_copto.jpg